PRAISE FOR

Soul by Soul

"*Soul by Soul* is a stunning achievement of both immersive reportage and rigorous research. With integrity, eloquence, and grace, Carranca tells the story of the secret networks of evangelical missionaries living and working in closed countries in the Muslim world, missionaries whose trust she earns over years of careful reporting in high-risk situations. At the same time, she traces the definitive history of the revolutionary transformation of Global Christianity and its mission from the Northern Hemisphere to the Global South. This is an extraordinary book."

ELIZA GRISWOLD,
Pulitzer Prize–winning author of *Amity and Prosperity: One Family and the Fracturing of America*

"Brazilian journalist Carranca makes her English-language debut with a riveting report on the 'secretive world' of evangelical Christian missionaries proselytizing to Muslims. . . . The result is a breathtaking deep dive into a clandestine, high-stakes world of clashing religions."

Publishers Weekly starred review

COLUMBIA GLOBAL REPORTS
NEW YORK

Soul by Soul

The Evangelical Mission to Spread the Gospel to Muslims

Adriana Carranca

Projected Annual Growth Rate of Country Populations, 2010–2050

- ≤-0.51%
- -0.50 to -0.01
- 0.00 to 0.99
- 1.00 to 1.99
- ≥ 2.00

SOURCE: The Future of World Religions: Population Growth Projections, 2010–2050
PEW RESEARCH CENTER

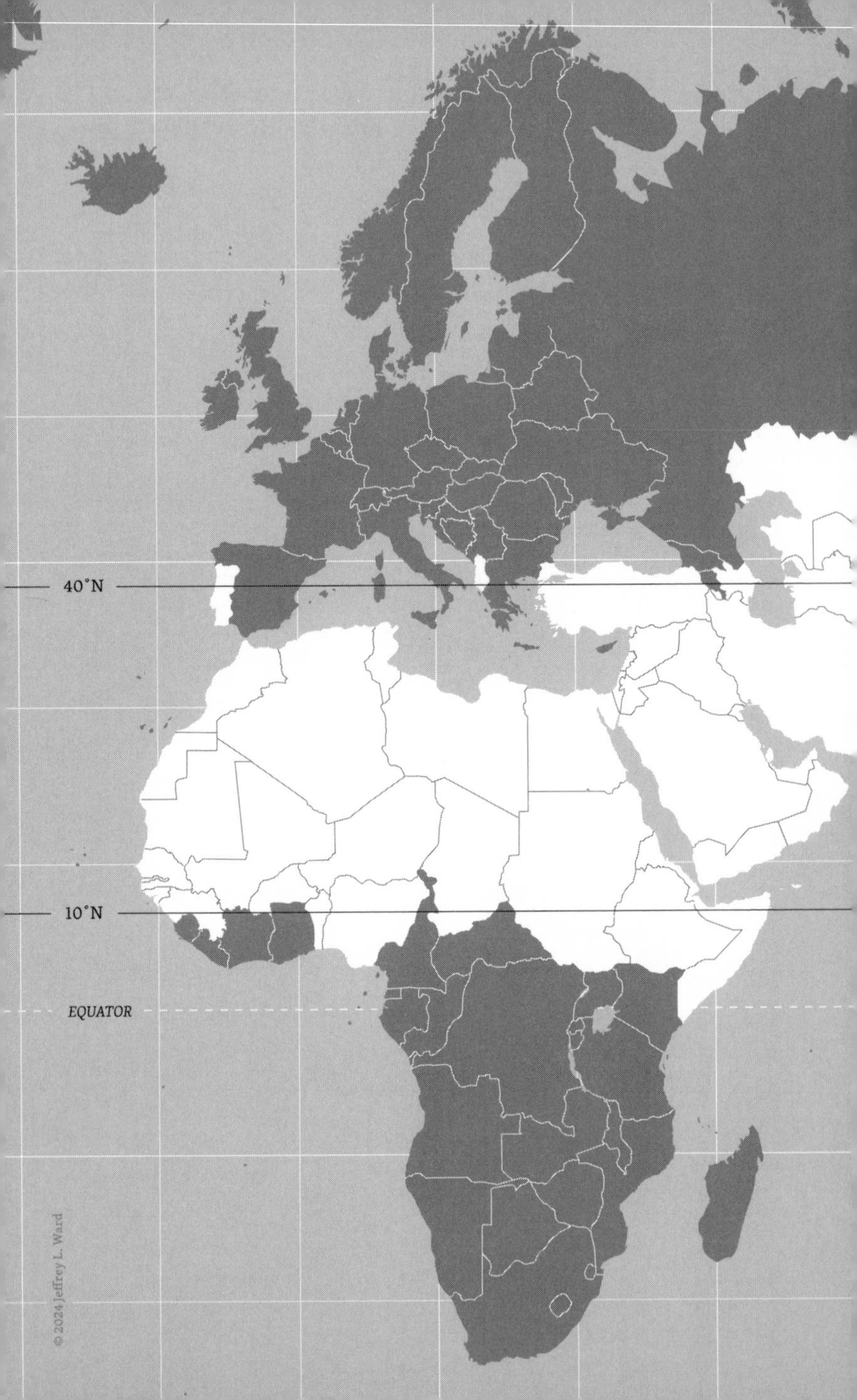
40°N
10°N
EQUATOR

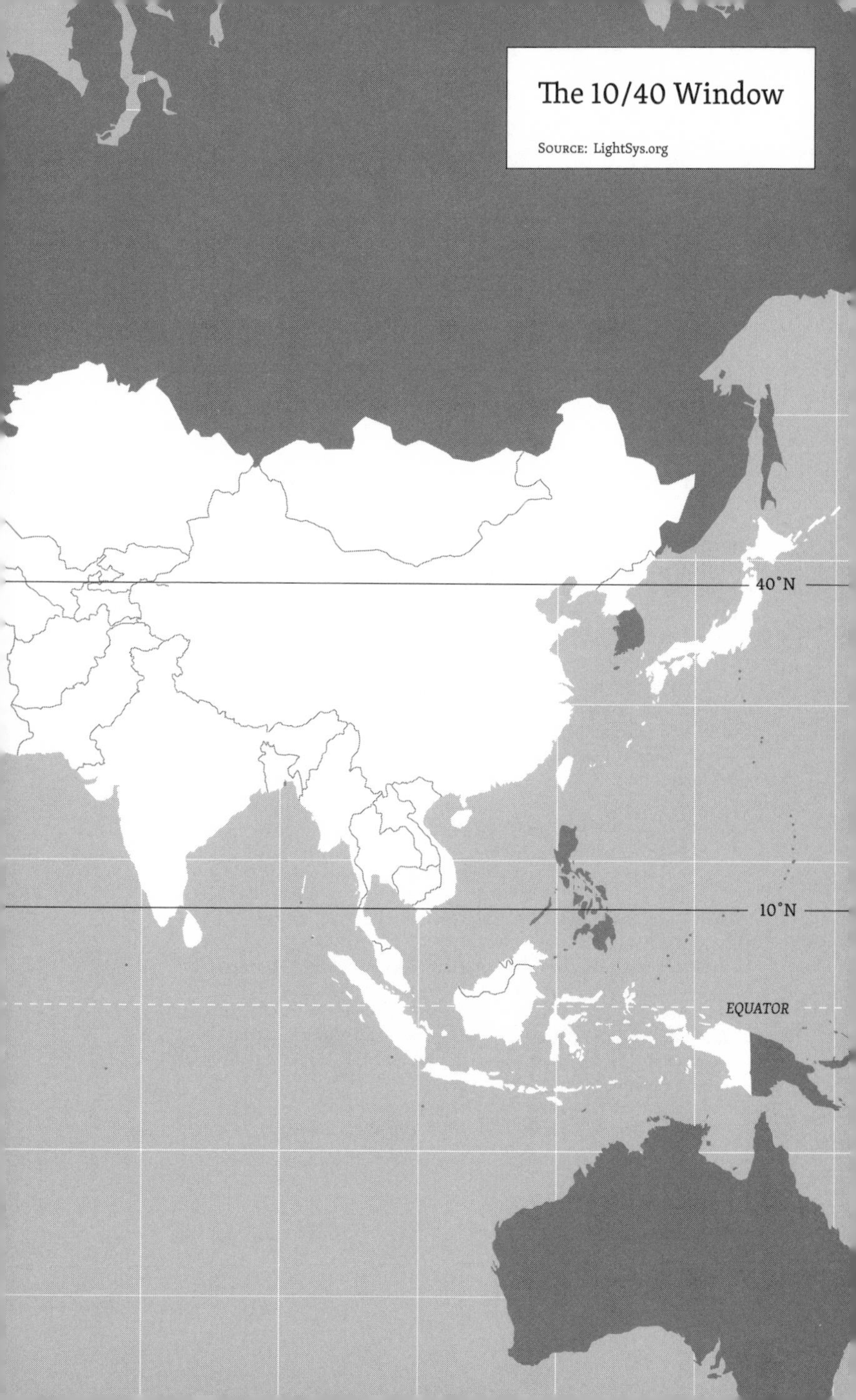
The 10/40 Window
Source: LightSys.org
40°N
10°N
EQUATOR

Published with support from the Andrew W. Mellon Foundation

Soul by Soul
The Evangelical Mission to Spread the Gospel to Muslims

Published by Columbia Global Reports
91 Claremont Avenue, Suite 515
New York, NY 10027
globalreports.columbia.edu
facebook.com/columbiaglobalreports
@columbiaGR

Library of Congress Cataloging-in-Publication Data
Names: Carranca, Adriana, author.
Title: Soul by soul : the Evangelical mission to spread the Gospel to Muslims / Adriana Carranca.
Description: New York, NY : Columbia Global Reports, [2024]
Includes bibliographical references.
Identifiers: LCCN 2022060267 (print) | LCCN 2022060268 (ebook) | ISBN 9798987053522 (paperback) | ISBN 9798987053539 (ebook)
Subjects: LCSH: Evangelicalism--Middle East--History--21st century. | Muslims--Middle East--21st century. | Conversions--Christianity--21st century.
Classification: LCC BR1642.M64 C37 2023 (print) | LCC BR1642.M64 (ebook) | DDC 230/.046240956--dc23/eng/20230515
LC record available at https://lccn.loc.gov/2022060267
LC ebook record available at https://lccn.loc.gov/2022060268

Book design by Strick&Williams
Map design by Jeffrey L. Ward
Author photograph courtesy of the author

Printed in the United States of America

To those whose faith in God—or no faith at all—
makes them better human beings

CONTENTS

American God

"John, we are gonna die today," Zeyad Zaid told his American comrade a little before they left Baghdad on a convoy carrying supplies to support US forces fighting insurgents in the Diyala Governorate, which stretches from the northeast of Iraq's capital to the border with Iran. Soldiers described Diyala as the most dangerous and "war-like" of the provinces, and bloodshed had been recurrent. "I know the area because this is my country," Zaid recalls having told John. "I am scared." The US soldier listened quietly, then removed his gold necklace with a cross pendant and put it around Zaid's neck. *Jesus will protect you.*

It was early 2007, the beginning of the troop surge that President George W. Bush announced on January 10. Zaid, then a twenty-two-year-old Sunni Muslim born in Baghdad, had been hired by a private contractor as a truck driver for the US Army in Iraq the year before. The vulnerability of the convoys had become apparent since the beginning of the war in 2003. Still, the surge deployed troops into even more dangerous terrains, resulting in the war's deadliest year for American soldiers. Casualties among civilians working for private contractors alongside the US military also soared to record levels.

Around Khan Bani Saad, the convoy—sixteen trucks driven by Iraqi contractors, escorted by five US Army Humvees—was caught in an ambush. The insurgents attacked with rocket-propelled grenades, road bombs, and snipers. Zaid remembers the sound of the massive explosions he had only seen before at the cinema in Baghdad: "It was like a *Star Wars* movie." Then, a roadside bomb exploded under his truck. He felt the force of the blast's shock wave. The next thing Zaid remembers, he was lying in a pool of blood inside the wrecked, overturned truck, and couldn't feel his legs. *I'm dying*, he thought.

American soldiers came to Zaid's rescue. They dragged him behind the walls of a nearby school, shielding themselves from the bullets flying over their heads. One of the soldiers placed tourniquets around Zaid's thighs to stop the bleeding and infused the area with topical antibiotics. "Don't sleep!" Zaid remembers the soldier shouting while slapping his face as he seemed to be losing consciousness. Zaid prayed to Allah.

The convoy was under relentless fire until a helicopter managed to access the area and lift Zaid to the US Air Force Theater Hospital at Balad Air Base, sixty-four kilometers north of Baghdad. The medical team informed Zaid that he would have to undergo surgery and that his legs might not be saved. Zaid begged the doctors not to cut off his legs. He had been a soccer prodigy as a child, and except for his physical strength, he had little left to rely on to support himself and his family. "Just let me die," he pleaded.

When a corpsman cut his clothing away to prepare him for the surgery, the team saw the pendant on his chest. "Are you a

Christian?" Zaid remembers a doctor asking. "I said yes. I knew Americans were Christians, so I thought they'd give me better medical treatment if I was a Christian too. At that point, I just wanted to stop them from cutting off my legs." The chaplain came to pray with him before the surgery, and Zaid passed out.

When Zaid woke up the next day, his legs had been saved, but he could no longer walk. Zaid stayed in bed at home in Diyala for nine months, writhing. "I would hit my head on the wall to pass out so I'd stop the pain," he told me. The war unfolding around him sometimes filled his bedroom with a noxious smell of chlorine, burned debris, and sweat that soaked the mattress following each explosion: the stench of fear.

"After nine months, I gave up. I had no hope. The war had destroyed my future and my family," Zaid said. "I wanted to kill myself." Zaid had grown resentful and disillusioned. He'd ask himself, Why is there no peace in this world? Why is God watching us dying here and doing nothing? In the years after the fall of Saddam Hussein's regime, religious and ethnic violence between Sunni and Shiite Muslims and between Arabs and Kurds intensified. In Iraq's battlefields, all sides showed their brutal worst, and Zaid blamed fellow Muslims for the carnage he witnessed and for his own fate. One thought grew increasingly intrusive in Zaid's mind: *I hate the God who made these people*.

It didn't occur to Zaid that the United States had started the war in Iraq based on a lie, nor that American Christians in general, and white evangelical Protestants in particular, were the biggest supporters of what came to be understood as an unprovoked military invasion. During his nine-month period serving the US military through a contractor, Zaid had grown fond of his comrade John. "Every time I talked to him, he always seemed so peaceful," he said. "I thought, maybe that's because he is Christian."

So, this time, Zaid decided to pray to the "American God."

Zaid was unfamiliar with how Christians prayed, so he began with, "I don't believe in You. But I will tell You something: If You are God, make me walk again, and I'll know You exist." He pleaded: "Please, God, make me walk again." Then one day, Zaid received a call. The caller introduced himself as a representative of a private contractor offering medical support in Iraq. Zaid argued that he wasn't eligible for health insurance. But, as Zaid remembers it, the man insisted that he come to Bagdad: *We want to help you walk again.*

In Baghdad, Zaid underwent two additional surgeries at the Al Jadriya Hospital followed by six months of intense physical therapy. Amazingly, the treatment worked. "I walked again, just a little bit, but . . ." Zaid stuttered, before breaking into tears. "But . . . I was so happy!"

Back home, he shared with his devout Muslim father some thoughts on how the war had made him question his faith. "He slapped me in the face and called me an infidel." (Even before his conversion, Shiite militiamen in his neighborhood had labeled Zaid an "infidel" before because he was raised a Sunni; so did Sunni associates of Al Qaeda, because he refused to join their ranks.) After his recovery, Zaid went to the south of Iraq and accepted an office job offer with another contractor, but that didn't last. "Working for the US Army in Iraq became very risky," he said. "People hate America. Once the local militias learned I worked for a contractor, they tried to kill me five times."

In June 2013, Zaid left Iraq. He entered Jordan with a temporary visa for medical treatment and never returned. There he learned of Christians assisting Syrian and Iraqi refugees in a small village near Amman, and came to them. More than three thousand men, women, and children crossed the border daily with battered bodies and broken spirits and the missionaries stood ready to offer them aid and eternal salvation. However, the evangelicals preaching the "American God" were not Americans, as Zaid would have expected. They turned out to be Brazilians, Colombians, Mexicans, South Africans, Chinese, and South Koreans.

A Brazilian pastor, Homero Azis, led the group. A "born-again" convert from the Roman Catholic Church, pastor Azis has an academic background in missiology (the study of religious missions) from the Bethel Theological Seminary, an affiliate of the Association for Evangelical Theological Education in Latin America, and in language studies from the Presbyterian Institute of Mackenzie, the first Protestant university in Latin America. He is a former minister of the country's first native Pentecostal church, O Brasil para Cristo, whose pastor was converted from Catholicism at the Assemblies of God and ordained by the International Church of the Foursquare Gospel. All of these institutions were started by US missionaries who brought about the evangelization of Latin America in the nineteenth century.

Azis first traveled to Jordan on a short-term mission with Portas Abertas, the Brazilian branch of California-headquartered mission organization Open Doors, advertised as "the world's largest outreach to persecuted Christians in the most high-risk places." In over seven years working for Open Doors, Azis claims to have smuggled around two hundred Latin American missionaries into thirty "closed countries"—all of them majority-Muslim countries, except North Korea.

In Jordan, Azis first joined Catholic priests and Protestant pastors in distributing food, clothes, and other essential items to refugees at the border with Syria. As the long-term needs of refugees became evident, he left Open Doors and moved to Jordan with his family to start a new permanent ministry named Al-Rahwa (it translates to Hope Church) in partnership with the Jordan Baptist Convention, established by American Southern Baptist missionaries with the aim of "winning Arabs for Christ."

It was June 2014, and the Islamic State of Iraq and Syria, a then largely unknown jihadist group with roots in Al Qaeda, had just made international headlines for declaring its "caliphate" over a seized area that would grow to the size of Great Britain and attract forty thousand foreign fighters from a hundred countries at the height of its power. The group destroyed churches, shrines, and historical sites as it advanced over Syrian and Iraqi territories. It killed scores of people, leaving behind a trail of beheaded, stoned, and crucified corpses.

The sudden emergence of ISIS propelled terrified Iraqis and Syrians to escape to neighboring countries in unprecedented numbers, causing a massive dislocation that raised the global number of people forcibly displaced by conflict or persecution to the highest recorded since World War II.

When I first met Azis in Jordan in 2018, he was preparing for the same journey the refugees had taken, only in the opposite direction. He was going to Mosul, Iraq's second-largest city and ISIS's last stronghold. Scores of dead bodies were being dug up from the ruins, and grueling battles were still unfolding in militant-held parts of the area. The Jordanian-Iraqi border was closed, so he flew to Turkey with another Brazilian missionary, and both got on a bus carrying $14,000 in cash stuffed in their pockets, shoes, and underwear.

The money was used to rebuild a house destroyed in the final Battle of Mosul. Another Iraqi "born-again" Christian baptized by Azis had donated the house to the ministry. It is located in Bartella, a historic Assyrian town on the outskirts of Mosul and home to Syriac Orthodox Christians, descendants of some of the early followers of Jesus. There, amid ruins, the Brazilian pastor inaugurated the first evangelical church of ancient Bartella.

Soul by Soul tells the story of the colossal efforts of American evangelicals to proclaim Christianity "to the ends of the Earth," a movement that triumphed in the Global South, challenged the Vatican, then turned east in full force to evangelize Muslims. In light of swelling anti-Americanism boosted by the US-led war on terror following the terrorist attacks of September 11 and the military campaigns in Afghanistan and Iraq, mission fields across the Middle East and South Asia turned into no-go zones. Sending North American missionaries could be suicidal, so Evangelists trained and equipped the new churches in the Southern Hemisphere, particularly Latin America, to fight for souls along Christian-Muslim fault lines.

I first heard of this on a reporting trip to Afghanistan in 2008, when a humanitarian worker told me about a Brazilian couple running a pizza delivery business in Kabul. Latin American missionaries were largely unheard of then, let alone in the Muslim world, so I suspected they were either poppy dealers or mercenaries. They lived in secrecy, for spreading Christianity in Afghanistan, as in most of the Muslim world, is illegal. Converting from Islam is considered apostasy, a crime punishable by death.

It took two years for S. P. Luiz to agree to talk, under the condition that I kept his complete name secret for safety reasons. We first met briefly at a café in São Paulo-Guarulhos International Airport shortly before he returned to Kabul. He seemed initially reluctant, and I thought our conversation would go nowhere. But, as the voice on the airport loudspeaker called the passengers for his flight, he looked deep into my eyes and finally blurted out, in a move that seemed to me like a miracle: "Do you want to know what I do in Afghanistan?" I did.

In the following years, Luiz granted me rare access to the secretive world of Christian missionaries evangelizing among Muslims. His journey took me to underground house churches in Afghanistan, among persecuted Christian converts in Pakistan, to a close-mouthed summit on global Evangelism in Indonesia, the world's largest Muslim country, and to mission fields in Egypt, Iraq, Jordan, Syria, and Turkey.

This isn't just Luiz's narrative but the story of a global movement. It is also a story of the twenty-first century—the century of religion. When church membership started to decline in the Northern Hemisphere in the aftermath of World War II, some quickly proclaimed we had entered a post-religion era. "Is God Dead?" asked *Time* magazine on an iconic cover page in 1966. Conversely, we saw an unexpected resurgence of religion as a significant force. Islam and Christianity are at an all-time high and continue growing—and clashing—in different parts of the globe.

The two countries with the largest population in the world are experiencing religious revivals: China is on a path to becoming the world's largest Christian nation by 2030, while Hinduism is thriving in India at the expense of a persecuted Muslim minority. Even the United States can hardly claim to have entered a post-religion era, given the Christian Right's emergence as a political power, as it is in parts of Europe. God isn't dead. God has gone global.

Christianity's shift to the Global South is the most dramatic dislocation of the center of the religion in its history. When the first World Missionary Conference was held in Edinburgh in 1910, 80 percent of all Christians lived in Europe and North America. By the time delegates met in Lausanne, Switzerland, for the first International Congress on World evangelization, in 1974, there were more Christians in the Global South than in the North for the first time in more than a millennium. By 2020, there were over 1.2 billion Christians in Latin America and sub-Saharan Africa alone—half of the world's 2.4 billion followers.

Christianity not only moved south but changed from within. The case of Brazil best exemplifies the shift. Though Brazil is still home to the world's largest Catholic population, the Vatican lost more followers there than in any other place—from 92 percent of the population in 1970 down to 50 percent in less than half a century—and most remain non-practicing. For those familiar with the changing global Christian landscape, the first Latin American pontiff's election was no surprise. Pope Francis is also a Jesuit, a member of the Society of Jesus, the Roman Church's missionary order.

Catholics still make up half of all Christians worldwide, Protestants make up 37 percent, and Orthodox Christians represent 12 percent. But Protestantism is growing faster. The force behind the trend is Pentecostalism, the charismatic religious movement that, in little more than a century beginning in 1906, evolved from a small group speaking in tongues in a shack on Azusa Street, in Los Angeles, California, to a worldwide movement with an estimated three hundred million followers. That makes it the fastest-growing religious sect in history and the only meaningful competitor to Islam, the world's fastest-growing religion.

In no other place has Pentecostalism grown faster than in Latin America, with about 70 percent of evangelicals identifying as Pentecostal in Brazil. A similar phenomenon occurred in Africa. In 2010, near the five hundredth anniversary of the Reformation, almost nine in ten of the world's Protestants lived outside of Europe, with more believers in Nigeria than in its birthplace, Germany. By 2040, more will live in Brazil than in the United States, home to roughly 20 percent of all Protestants.

Protestantism was brought to the new world by immigrant Englishmen, mostly Puritans, who crossed the Atlantic on a mission to build a New England where they hoped to begin establishing the Kingdom of God on Earth. By the nineteenth century, virtually all Protestants in America believed it was their duty to spread the gospel at home and abroad. This is where this book began. It departed from my own inquiry on why American Protestants came to see themselves as God's ambassadors.

While Americans still dispatch more missionaries than any other country, Brazil has become the second largest sender, followed by South Korea, India, South Africa, the Philippines, Mexico, China, Colombia, and Nigeria. By 2021, more than 200,000 foreign missionaries (around 47 percent of the world's total) were being sent from the Global South, up from 31,000 (or 12 percent) in 1970. Christianity's shift toward the Southern

Hemisphere became visible in the World Religions Map and the global missions movement.

Though geographically broad in scope, my reporting looks at the global mission movement through the lens of a Latin American itinerant believer. As a reporter, I wanted to see how the dynamics of soul-winning played on the ground. I wanted to understand what could lead a middle-class educated father to leave everything behind and move to a distant, war-torn country with his wife and two small children to share his faith. What I found was a booming global missionary movement that has shaped Christianity North and South, turned East to convert Muslims, and forged something called World Christianity.

It can look like this: A Brazilian pastor leading missionaries from Colombia, Mexico, South Africa, China, and South Korea serving among Arab refugees across the Middle East in partnership with a Jordanian Baptist pastor, but also at times alongside Eastern Orthodox and Roman Catholics, with financial support provided mainly by American evangelicals, as well as an Irish charity, a South African NGO, and loyal members of small congregations in South America. And their converts from Islam are circling back to Europe and the United States to preach among fellow refugees. By doing so, these new believers are enlarging the church's flock and reviving Christianity in the West.

As a secular journalist, maintaining my objectivity while navigating the subjectivity of faith was undoubtedly the biggest challenge. At some point, I made peace with it. When S. P. Luiz and his wife, Gis, asked me, as they often did: "Do you believe?" I answered: "I believe that you believe." That much was true.

Prologue

As it goes in the New Testament, the resurrected Jesus appeared to the Apostles on a hillside in Galilee and there gave them the final instructions—known as the Great Commission—to "go and make disciples of all nations." Before long, in Jerusalem, the Holy Spirit descended upon them, and they "began to speak with other tongues." Jewish pilgrims "out of every nation under heaven" celebrating the Feast of Pentecost were amazed to hear, each in their own language, the Apostles share the good news. Three thousand were baptized. The day of Pentecost marks the birth of the Christian church. From there, these early disciples of Jesus moved in different directions to spread His teachings, launching the global missions movement.

Christianity has never been a homogeneous religion. The Apostles each preached to a particular ethnic group of the vast Roman Empire—Hebrews, Greeks, Hellenists, Romans, Samaritans, Phoenicians, Syrians, and other Near Eastern communities. The emerging Christian fellowships developed distinctive theologies and worship practices, competed with one another, and disputed different interpretations of Jesus's message. Initial controversies led to the Jerusalem Council, which exempted the gentiles from adhering to Jewish traditions maintained in early Christianity in favor of an inclusive faith.

In the following centuries, laypeople continued to spread Christian beliefs secretly through personal connections—in conversations with neighbors, friends, and family members. Persecution conversely facilitated Christianity's spread through forced migration. It was only in the fourth century that Christians gained legal rights and Christianity became the state religion of Rome, allowing it to further spread and prosper. After the fall of Rome, Christianity was a unifying, but not a uniform, force. Islam rose in the seventh century as a powerful opponent in the Middle East while Christianity spread farther West, entangled with the expansion of the European powers. Emboldened by a sense of moral superiority, Christian Europeans sought to "save" native peoples—and eventually the world.

Professor Brian Stanley, an authority in World Christianity, cites the Puritan settlers in New England as the best example of the Christian European thought of the time. The first Puritans who crossed the Atlantic on board the *Arbella*, in 1630, saw themselves on a mission to redeem Christendom. They believed that the aggravating political, economic, and social disorder at home was caused by God's wrath. Unable to reform the Church of England, they ventured into the wilderness in hope of building a godly commonwealth. Such a model society would prove God's blessing upon the Puritan experiment and multiply, advancing His Kingdom until all humanity was brought under God's law as "one flock and one Sheppard."

The first Bible ever printed in America was not in English but in Algonquin, the language of the natives whom these settlers sought to evangelize. The converted were expected to speak English, dress like Englishmen, and practice English Christian traditions. They lived in praying towns where civilization and salvation were provided hand in hand. The efforts of these pioneering missionaries in America, notably John Eliot, led to the Act for the Promoting and Propagating the Gospel of Jesus Christ in New England, passed by the English Parliament in 1649. It created a spearhead ecumenical coalition between Anglicans, reformers, and dissenters to support proselytizing efforts in the colonies.

The First Great Awakening helped make a nation by giving Americans living in dispersed colonies a common evangelical identity. Itinerant preachers on horseback filled the spiritual needs of the unchurched, and accelerated soul-winning. By the turn of the nineteenth century, nearly a million people had made their way west of the Blue Ridge, and these preachers followed them, bringing the church to the irreligious new frontiers. Camp meetings gathered isolated settlers in communion for days, or even weeks, during which the preachers performed Christian rites like baptisms, marriages, and funerals, sang hymns, and danced. The intensity of the worship often led to the collective ecstasy that ignited the Second Great Awakening—a purely US-bred revival that spread across America and evolved into a new form of evangelical culture.

During the revivals, on a Saturday in August 1806, five students at Williams College met for their regular reading and praying section at a grove of maple trees north of the campus. Showers and thunderstorms forced them to take shelter in a haystack. There they prayed to God to lead them through the waters into foreign mission fields. Soon after, the students formed the Society of the Brethren. It later moved to the Andover Seminary, the first graduate school in North America, where they met Adoniram Judson. Together the group petitioned the Congregationalist leadership to establish a mission-sending body, and the American Board of Commissioners for Foreign Missions (ABCFM) was born in 1810. It was America's first Christian Protestant missions agency.

Two years later, eight American missionaries commissioned by the board sailed to India. Judson, Luther Rice, and others in the group are widely regarded as the first Americans to go on a mission overseas. In fact, an emancipated slave named George Liele preceded them as the first known American and Baptist missionary to any land. Liele was converted by his enslaver and began preaching in the plantations of Savannah, Georgia, where he started the first African American Baptist Church in the United States. Liele later fled to Jamaica to avoid reenslavement and to "pursue God's call." When Judson and Rice arrived in India, Liele had served in Jamaica for three decades, preached in plantations and homes, baptized hundreds—some white men and women included—established free schools for Black children run by Black deacons, and founded the first Baptist Church in Kingston.

Nevertheless, Judson was among the first missionaries commissioned by an organized mission agency, the American Board. The mission in India was short-lived. The East India Company saw missionaries as destabilizing and denied them residence. The missionaries left Calcutta for nearby lands, while Rice returned home to lobby for the mission cause. On

March 15, 1813, Rice embarked on a Portuguese vessel bound for the US with a stop in the port of São Salvador da Bahia de Todos os Santos, or the Holy Savior of the Bay of All Saints, in northeast Brazil. He stayed for two months as a guest of the US consul, according to Rice's memoir, "to reconnoiter South America as a missionary field." Rice described Salvador as "about as bad a state of heathenism as any," which he blamed on Catholic superstition. "Not a religious person could I find in the place," he wrote, adding that "a missionary of righteousness might do some good in that country."

In the US, Rice advocated for financial support to the mission in Asia, but also recommended that "missionaries should be sent to South America." In a letter to Congregationalists, he expressed convictions that only those who demonstrated faith should receive baptism. This conviction led Rice to become a Baptist (as did the Judsons, who had moved as missionaries to Burma) and to organize the US's first national Baptist Society. Methodists and Presbyterians soon formed their own mission boards. The individualistic essence of salvation embodied in the spirit of the nineteenth-century evangelical revivals stirred a paradigm shift in missionary thinking that would transform Catholic-majority Latin America into a legitimate mission field. In the eyes of the revived American evangelicals, being a Christian no longer sufficed—one had to be "born again."

The Second Great Awakening propelled US missions to Latin America. The American Bible Society began working in South America soon after its foundation in 1816, and two years later, a precursor of the Wycliffe Bible Translators started in Argentina. ABCFM first sent missionaries to Brazil in 1835. They were Methodists, Presbyterians, and Baptists, but they all shared a theological horizon characterized as evangelical, and halfway through the century, the values of America's revivals could be observed in Brazil.

Between 1810 and 1860, the ABCFM sent out sent out 2,000 missionaries, of whom 1,200 served at home in the United States. The "winning of the West" led ministers to concentrate on evangelizing and "civilizing" natives, Hispanic and African Americans, and immigrants. The controversies over slavery jeopardized any attempts at unity, and the Civil War brought missions to a halt.

Toward the end of the Civil War, Southern Confederate exiles started arriving in Mexico, Central America, and South America, searching for refuge, land for agriculture, and an unpaid labor force. Brazil was a particularly attractive destination. It was the last country in the Western world to abolish slavery, more than two decades after the end of the American Civil War. The Confederates first saw South America as a dark, heathen land. But the writings of the pioneer missionaries to the subcontinent offered them another way of looking at it. Many, such as the *Emigration Reporter* published by Presbyterian minister W. C. Emerson, or *Brazil and the Brazilians,* by James C. Fletcher and Daniel P. Kidder (respectively a Presbyterian and a Methodist), devoted pages to issues like commerce and agriculture.

Emerson later returned to the US as an agent of the Brazilian government to recruit Southerners for the colonies, while Fletcher became acting secretary of the American Legation in Brazil, in which position he induced the government to establish a regular steamship route between Rio de Janeiro and New York, which provided transportation to thousands of Confederate immigrants. In Brazil, Emperor Pedro II initiated an international campaign to attract Confederate farmers to his empire, hoping to develop agriculture. The government set up agencies across the Bible Belt and offered free relocation, cheap land, and tax subsidies. As many as twenty thousand Confederates took the offer.

Those were not the first Protestants to land in South America. The very first mission of the Reformed Church anywhere outside Europe dates back to 1555, when a group of mostly Huguenots arrived at the shores of Guanabara Bay in Rio de Janeiro. However, South America was part of Roman Christendom, and the religious environment only began to change after the region's independence from the Spanish and Portuguese.

In an attempt to reconstruct an American way of life in Brazil, the Confederate exiles established congregations and asked denominations in the United States to send American pastors to preach in the colonies. The first Baptist church in Brazil was organized by Confederates in Santa Bárbara do Oeste, in the southeast state of São Paulo, in 1871. Worried about adequate schooling for their children, they sought "a school for every church."

Though not originally a Christian mission enterprise, the Confederates established the first Protestant churches, schools, and organizations in Latin America, preparing the terrain for the wave of missionaries who would bring about the evangelization of the subcontinent in the second half of the nineteenth century. To this day, Confederate flags adorn the graves in the American Cemetery in Santa Bárbara D'Oeste. Soldiers' descendants gather in the city saloons to the sound of Johnny Cash and battle songs like "Stonewall Jackson's Way" to celebrate the anniversary of the end of the Civil War.

In the years after the end of the conflict, foreign missions from America remained limited. That began to change after the Spanish-American War. Evangelicals saw the United States' emergence as a world power as a sign of divine Providence. Following the victory against Spain, the US took the Philippines, Puerto Rico, Guam, and Cuba as spoils of war, annexed Hawaii, and extended its influence in South America. America's advances and the development of the radio, the telegraph, and the steamship gave missionaries access to world peoples. By the end of the nineteenth century, Americans were convinced they had a mandate from God to spread Christianity anywhere in the world.

In July 1886, Dwight L. Moody, a well-known evangelist and the president of the Chicago branch of the Young Men's Christian Association (YMCA), convened students across the country for the first national Summer Bible Conference in the United States. Founded in London in a period of rapid industrialization, the YMCA aimed at providing young Christians working and serving away from home lodging and a safe refuge from the temptations of the secular world. In American cities, the YMCA opened dorms, lodges, and clubs; it promoted sports and personal development. The organization founded delegations in colleges and seminaries that multiplied in the nineteenth century with the increased demand for new ministers and missionaries in westward frontiers and urban areas.

For four weeks that year, 251 student delegates from eighty-nine universities and colleges in the United States and Canada gathered at the Mount Hermon School, founded by Moody in Northfield, Massachusetts. Addressing the young audience, Presbyterian Arthur Tappan Pierson, a catalyst for American foreign missions, urged, "All should go and go to all." By the last day of the conference, one hundred young men had signed a declaration affirming: "It is my purpose, if God permits, to become a foreign missionary."

In the aftermath of the conference, the "Mount Hermon One Hundred," as they came to be known, rallied campuses nationwide and YMCA's vast network of intercollegiate associations to recruit more students for missions. From that emerged the Student Volunteer Movement. Evangelizing Catholic Latin America concerned the movement's leadership from the beginning. Globally, some twenty thousand university students responded to the call to serve overseas under Pierson's watchword, "the evangelization of the world in this generation."

In the summer of 1910, Christian delegates convened in Edinburgh, Scotland, for the first World Missionary Conference. The key figure of the conference was John R. Mott, an American Methodist layperson and leader of both the Student Volunteer Movement for Foreign Missions and the World Student Christian Federation, who chaired the conference's proceedings. The meeting was, above all, a call for ecumenical collaboration. The nineteenth century had been an era of spectacular geographic advance and growth for Protestant missions. In the global mission field, competition was counterproductive. Worse still, it could expose a divided Kingdom of God.

Among the 1,215 delegates, more than a thousand were from the United States and Great Britain, and 169 came from continental Europe. Neither the Orthodox nor the Roman Catholic

Church sent representatives. The conference also failed to have one or two natives from mission lands. "Are we actually planting new churches or merely perpetuating mission?" British deacon Roland Allen, a former missionary to China, questioned. The American hegemony within the Protestant missionary movement was as evident as the Western sense of superiority. "Too often you promise us thrones in heaven but will not offer us chairs in your drawing rooms," said Bishop Vedanayagam Samuel Azariah, the first Indian bishop of the Anglican Communion.

The Anglican Church had conditioned its participation to two demands. First, that doctrine should not be discussed, which wouldn't be a problem since initiatives like the SVM had been held together on such a principle. Second, that all territories under the Roman Catholic Church were excluded as mission fields, so as not to upset the Vatican. That was a heavy blow for a movement founded on God's commission to "make disciples of all nations."

Backstage in Edinburgh, Robert Speer, perhaps the most enthusiastic representative of the Student Volunteer Movement to advocate for missions to Latin America, convened two unofficial parallel sessions to defend the cause. As the secretary of the Presbyterian Board of Foreign Missions, which he served for forty-six years, Speer toured dozens of churches in South America and returned on fire for evangelizing the region. Though he avoided direct criticism of the Catholic Church, Speer considered the moral conditions in the subcontinent irreligious. "The day has come," Speer said, "for us to take up our obligation to these Latin American peoples."

Three years later, Speer convened delegates in New York to discuss what was next for Latin America. He noted that its controversial exclusion from the World Missionary Conference conversely brought unprecedented attention to the region, and he summoned like-minded evangelists to use the momentum for a missionary impulse to the subcontinent. The group formed the Committee on Cooperation in Latin America, with Speer as the chairman. They designed a plan to reclaim Latin America's place in Evangelism.

Then, World War I broke out. All warring powers except for the Ottoman Empire were Christians. When the war ended, the idea of a Western higher morality was over, with long-lasting consequences for World Christianity.

On one side, some American evangelicals remained unshaken in their commitment to the liberal ideals of Christian ecumenic cooperation, and they put it to the test by joining the war relief efforts with more than prayers. These leaders were postmillennialists, believing that Christian missions were a way to advance peace and justice in the world, establishing God's Kingdom on Earth so Jesus could return. The concept of internationalism based on self-determination, equality, and cooperation following World War I and the peace treaties signed by the states gave them hope of establishing an international covenant based on the idea that one world needs one Church.

However, for another group of American evangelicals, the war showed that liberals were powerless to reform society, and they used that to prove postmillennialism wrong. To them, the Great War had opened the pages of prophetic Scripture. They saw the Bolshevik Revolution as the rise of the Beast and the Soviet Union as the northern empire to be defeated in Armageddon. The disintegration of the Ottoman Empire fueled premillennialism and added urgency to God's command to make disciples of all nations. They called on evangelicals to return to the fundamentals of the faith.

Then came World War II.

In 1947, a young evangelist named Billy Graham began traveling the United States on an itinerant ministry that attracted unprecedented crowds. Born in 1918 in Charlotte, North Carolina, Graham grew up on a two-hundred-acre farm and tuned into evangelical radio programs such as *Fuller's Old Fashioned Revival Hour*. He attended religious schools and spent Sundays at the conservative Associate Reformed Presbyterian Church. At sixteen, Graham was "born again" during a revival meeting. He was ordained a Southern Baptist minister at twenty-one and pursued further religious studies at Wheaton College, then known as the "Fundamentalist Harvard." There he met his wife, Ruth Bell, the daughter of conservative southern Presbyterian missionaries to China, where she grew up.

As an enthusiastic preacher, Graham kept a distance from the fundamentalist versus modernist divide, and focused on massive evangelism. Two world wars and the threat of a third, nuclear war, had revived premillennialist convictions while prophecies gained a new momentum. Graham's crusades framed the Cold War as the End Times final battle between Christ and the anti-Christ, and good versus evil. It was an appealing message. In 1952, Graham held a revival in Washington, DC, and spoke to some one hundred legislators on the steps of the Capitol. Soon after, he met President

Dwight D. Eisenhower, and the two became close. "Either communism must die, or Christianity must die because it is a battle between Christ and anti-Christ," Graham famously stated. From the point of view of Eisenhower, a religious revival couldn't be timelier.

Graham spoke to millions of Americans as he held crusades in almost every major city in the country, while his weekly radio program reached even more. His column, "My Answer," appeared in seventy-three newspapers. He took his crusades around the world two years later, and he visited South America twice in 1962. That October, the Cuban Missile Crisis brought the world to the brink of a nuclear war. The American preacher, who had met with Cuban dictator Fulgencio Batista in Havana before the dictator had been overthrown by Fidel Castro's revolutionary forces, was leading the closing service at San Lorenzo soccer stadium in Argentina when the arms-laden flotilla left Cuban shores, ending the crisis. He commented: "Some mission leaders now have reason to regret that they did not take Cuba more seriously during the years of opportunity. They now realize that the island nation constituted their nearest foreign mission field, yet was neglected."

The Catholic Church had just announced the Second Vatican Council, "a new Pentecost," which would equip the church for a new era of foreign missions. Vatican II made the College of Cardinals more representative of the church worldwide, placed unprecedented emphasis on the laity's apostolate, and encouraged private Bible reading and using the vernacular in the liturgy. It re-centered the church away from the Vatican and closer to "the people of God," calling upon this international fellowship to make disciples of all nations under the leadership of the bishops—the descendants of the Apostles. It was a turning point for the Catholicism, fostering its most significant reforms in almost two millennia.

Some scholars see Vatican II as a reaction to the evangelical surge in its stronghold of Latin America driven by Pentecostalism. The origins of Pentecostalism can be traced to a revival led by African American holiness preacher William Seymour at a vacated tumbledown shack on Azusa Street in Los Angeles, in 1906. Born in Louisiana to former enslaved parents, Seymour attracted a unique crowd of Americans and immigrants, rich and poor, Black and white, in a segregated America, all bonded by a sense of spiritual equality and unity.

Pentecostals didn't plan to start a new denomination. However, conservatives in the US largely view manifestations of the supernatural as heresies. They judged Pentecostalism an illegitimate sect and expelled pastors and parishioners who practiced it. Some founded new churches, while others became missionaries.

One of the leaders of the Azusa Street movement, Italian American missionary Louis Francescon, arrived in South America in 1909. He founded Assembleias Cristianas and Congregação Cristã, the first Pentecostal churches in Argentina and Brazil, respectively. That same year, a minister prophesied to two Swedish Baptist immigrants that they would become missionaries in Pará. Gunnar Vingren and Daniel Berg had never heard of the place, so they ran to a nearby library and learned of a state by that name in northern Brazil. Coincidentally, a ship would depart from New York to Belém, the state capital, in two weeks. In Belém, Vingren focused on evangelism, while Berg supported the two as a metalworker. They initially joined the local Baptist church. As their Portuguese improved, the missionaries started an independent Pentecostal church named Missão da Fé Apostolíca, with just eighteen members. In 1918, the church became an affiliate of the Assemblies of God Church in North America, giving birth to the Assembleia de Deus in Brazil. As of 2020, its membership totaled twenty-two million, making it the world's largest Assembly of God.

Pentecostals believe that the gifts of the spirit given to the Apostles are still available to all believers. While initially ostracized in the US, the movement received a warm welcome in Latin America. Pentecostals appealed to and welcomed the poor and the illiterate with festive services, spiritually intense worships that legitimated existing indigenous spiritual practices, promises of healing, and testimonies of a life-transforming faith. It gave adherents a higher sense of belonging, as anyone could be empowered by the Holy Spirit and become a church leader. In the 1940s, only a few Pentecostal denominations had been allowed in the National Association of Evangelicals. By the 1980s, half of all Latin American Protestants were Pentecostals.

Influenced by Pentecostalism, the Roman Catholic Church had its own charismatic movement beginning in the sixties. Pentecostals (in fact, evangelicals in general) were influenced by Catholic reformist movements that emerged in the context of Latin American struggles, particularly liberation theology. Its central principle is a special concern for the poor as part of Christian obligation. Adherents formed the *communidades eclesyasticas de base,* grassroots groups of Catholic priests and laypeople dedicated to meet the spiritual and the immediate needs of parishioners. (A decade later, there were an estimated one hundred thousand communities in Brazil.)

In 1968, delegates of the liberal ecumenic World Council of Churches gathered in Uppsala, Sweden, and called for redirecting missions away from Evangelism to focus on social change (if necessary, through revolution). Conservative American evangelicals were alarmed. In response to the liberal theologies nurtured within the WCC, the Billy Graham Evangelistic Association the next year sponsored the First Latin American Congress for Evangelization (CLADE, in its Spanish acronym), an early attempt to counter the influence and "the dangers of Marxist-inflected theologies" in the subcontinent.

Billy Graham and his aides started formulating plans for their own world conference dedicated to promoting global Evangelism, with all participants being "totally and thoroughly evangelical." The American preacher had become a world celebrity, and felt the pressure that came with it. Graham was increasingly challenged to come out against the evils of the time, including racism in the United States, the Vietnam War, South Africa's apartheid, and brutal military regimes in South America. Graham was well aware of the trends in World Christianity, and the divergences between the North and the South. He also recognized that the future of the Christian faith was no longer in America. To US evangelists, taking the reins of global Evangelism was a matter of faith and survival.

The International Congress on World Evangelization, sponsored by the Billy Graham Evangelistic Association, was held in Lausanne, Switzerland, in the summer of 1974. Participation was by invitation only, national quotas were established, and scholarships were offered to guarantee the plurality and geographic representation of the conference delegates. It was previously agreed that representatives of the younger churches should be involved from the outset to ensure that their demands would be addressed for the benefit of "the church's entire mission." In total, four thousand participants and guests attended. They came from 150 countries and 135 Protestant denominations.

In his opening evening address at Lausanne, Graham cheered the visibility and energy of "younger churches" as he stood before a multinational and racially diverse crowd. But the joyful mood didn't last long. Speaking on the first day, purposely in Spanish, Ecuadoran evangelist René Padilla caused a stir when he openly attacked American forms of "culture Christianity," which, in his view, reduced religion into a marketed product and viewed converts merely as numbers. He declared that such a vision could "only be the basis for unfaithful churches, for strongholds of racial and class discrimination."

Samuel Escobar, of Peru, was the second Latin American to speak, attracting as much attention at the conference. He warned against making Christianity the ideology of the West, just as communism had become the ideology of the Eastern bloc. Escobar reminded the audience that many of the countries that had succumbed to violent Marxist revolutions were those where Christianity had allowed itself to be identified with the ruling class. That was a direct attack against American evangelical leaders, Graham among them.

The third radical voice at Lausanne, a young evangelist from Puerto Rico named Orlando Costas, rendered the message of Padilla and Escobar still more explicit. "American evangelical missionary support," he said, "is tainted by links to imperialistic culture and vested economic interests."

The criticisms voiced by Padilla, Escobar, and Costas were not a surprise. The radicals, as they became known, had been challenging the top-down approach of North American evangelicals to South America. In response to Graham's conservative CLADE, which they mocked as "made in the USA," Padilla, Escobar, and like-minded Latinos had formed the Fraternidad Teológica Latinoamericana, an evangelical alternative to liberation theology. Central to the radicals' thinking was the purely Latin American "misión integral," a strand of theology developed by Padilla since the 1950s, which added social responsibility to the gospel. But the Lausanne Congress was perhaps the first time that such criticism was brought to the center stage of world Evangelism.

Perhaps more surprising to US delegates at Lausanne was the fact that the Latin American radicals weren't alone. That became evident when Padilla's "provocative" speech, as *Time* magazine put it, received "the longest round of applause," according to *Crusade Magazine*. Supporters included African delegates who had been calling for a moratorium on US missions, which they considered "patronizing," in favor of self-determination. During the conference, Padilla, Escobar, Costas, and allies called delegates to a parallel meeting aimed at drafting a proposal to be considered in the Lausanne Covenant. To their surprise, some five hundred attended.

Soon the assembly parted into two groups: those led by the United States, who wanted to retain a focus on Evangelism, and the young "radicals" led by Latin Americans, who demanded broader attention to social concern. *Christianity Today* described the division as between the "data-oriented church growth school and the discipleship-demanding compassion and justice group."

The radicals of the Global South fought the American conservatives to add amendments to the Lausanne Covenant. The strong hand of the traditionalists showed through the final document. Still, the radicals also succeeded in some of their proposed amendments, including the covenant's main statement: "We rejoice that a new missionary era has dawned. The dominant role of western missions is fast disappearing." Though the document didn't mention the word *moratorium*, it did recommend a reduction in foreign missionaries. "Missions have all too frequently exported with the gospel an alien culture," the covenant read, suggesting that the sending of American missionaries be replaced by training and supporting national leaders in Latin America, Africa, and Asia.

Conservatives, on the other hand, made sure to include in the final text that neither is "social action evangelism nor is political liberation salvation." Nevertheless, the delegates agreed to affirm "that evangelism and socio-political involvement are both part of our Christian duty." In the end, a consensus had been reached, and most of the official delegates signed the Lausanne Covenant's final text.

The global multicultural community presented at Lausanne changed the future of Christianity. It marked the rise of leadership and influence from the Global South and a broader turn toward a more holistic mission model. With time, however, US conservatives would remodel "holistic mission" away from emphasis on social action as an integral part of Evangelism to social action as a means to evangelize. The real achievement at Lausanne was an agreement on what global Christianity meant: almost homogeneously conservative in traditional morality and social mores but ethnically, racially, culturally, and generationally diverse; more inclusive of different economic classes, divergent in opinions, and multifaceted in perceptions of the world. Evangelicalism progressively transformed from a tradition shaped by Anglo-American conservative Protestant perspectives into a multicultural global Christian family.

The Lausanne Conference is widely regarded as the most significant gathering in the history of the evangelical church. There, the delegates designed the theological framework and action plan to convert the world to Christianity in the twenty-first century. The global spread of the gospel didn't start at Lausanne in 1974, but, as historian Melani McAlister notes: "The terms of the next forty years were set there, as evangelicals turned, heart and soul, toward the world."

When the Latin American leaders at the Lausanne Congress returned home, there were only 136 Latin American missionaries abroad, of whom 105 were Brazilians. In the next three decades, this number would grow to the tens of thousands, with the first Latin American missions agency launched two years after the congress. But the division exposed in Lausanne continued. In 1982, liberal ecumenic Protestants formed the Latin American Council of Churches (CLAI), aimed at fostering both Evangelism and social change in the region. American conservatives, however, were suspicious of the organization's ties with the WCC, and that same year formed the Latin American Evangelical Consultation (CONELA), deepening the divide between ecumenical and evangelical, left and right, liberationists and evangelicals, with no "third ways" accepted.

The father of CONELA was the Argentinian Evangelist Luis Palau, exalted as the Spanish-speaking Latino version of

Billy Graham. Palau was Graham's translator for twenty years before becoming president of the Overseas Crusades (currently OC International). In 1978, using $100,000 in seed money from Graham, he started his own Luis Palau Association, based in Oregon, which claims that Palau preached to thirty million people in seventy-five countries. Like his mentor, Palau drew criticism for backing Latin American dictators like Guatemala's Efraín Ríos Montt—a "model" to Palau. A critic of liberation theology, Palau saw social responsibility as compromising the evangelical faith with left-wing ideology. CONELA adopted the Lausanne Covenant, but it had a clear focus on Evangelism.

As a branch of the World Evangelical Alliance, CONELA claimed to represent twenty million evangelicals, though the number has been contested. Most importantly, CONELA counted on like-minded American allies. With growing support and funding, it became a major force. A fellow countryman and pupil of Palau, Argentinian evangelist Luis Bush, was appointed as chairman of CONELA's Church Growth Commission.

Born in Argentina and raised in Brazil, Bush moved to the United States in the mid-sixties to study economics at the University of North Carolina. He worked in consulting for Arthur Andersen in Chicago before graduating from the Dallas Theological Seminary in 1977 and becoming a full-time missionary. The next year, Bush moved with his wife and two children to El Salvador to serve with the Central American Mission (CAM), founded by American fundamentalist theologian C. I. Scofield (the author of the annotated Bible that popularized dispensationalism), to spread the gospel in the region.

Soon, a brutal civil war broke out, which would last for twelve years, during which Bush founded the El Salvadoran Bible Institute and the country's first interdenominational agency, the Salvadoran Evangelical Mission, sent national missionaries overseas, and sponsored the first congress for young people of Central America in El Salvador. At the opening ceremony, as the first guest speaker came to the pulpit, a bomb exploded, "and it all went dark," he told me. Bush didn't think of leaving the country. Instead, he interpreted the event as God shaking Latin America to open the way to transcultural missions.

As the head of CONELA's Church Growth Commission, Bush built connections that bridged evangelicals in the United States and Latin America. That led him to organize the first Ibero-American Missions Congress, which met in 1987 in São Paulo, Brazil. More than three thousand delegates from every Latin American country and all around the world attended the first COMIBAM. There, Bush prophesized that Latin America would turn "from a mission field to a mission force." Recognizing that the Latin American church did not have the resources of its North American counterparts, Guatemalan pastor Rudy Giron anticipated that missions from Latin America would be "sacrificial." Nevertheless, in the following years, Bush worked with leaders of the global missions movement to make his prophecy become real. "He'd rally the global network of Spanish and Portuguese speaking nations, train national church leaders, and connect them with evangelicals worldwide," the late American Evangelist Roberta Winter, co-founder of the US Center for World Mission, stated at Mission Frontiers. "Largely due to Luis Bush and others like him, Latin American evangelicals may very well become some of the great mission mobilizers of the world and take the lead in the Third World in the final countdown to the End of History."

On July 11, 1989, a torch that was first lit over a year before, and had been carried through fifty countries, arrived to a standing ovation at the Philippine International Convention Center, in Manila. It was the opening night of the Second International Conference on World Evangelization, or Lausanne II, an event with as many global ambitions as the Olympic Games. Music in more than twenty different languages was played over the loudspeakers. More than sixty Soviet Christian converts received a rousing welcome after being held at the airport in Moscow for two days. A Chinese pastor brought tears to the delegates' eyes as he recounted how he sang the gospel hymn "I Come to the Garden Alone" while in a Chinese prison. In total, 3,586 participants from 186 countries gathered for 10 days, attended some 400 workshops, listened to 47 primary addresses, and formed over 300 partnerships, networks, and new ministries. The conference also cost $10.5 million.

On opening night, Luis Bush rocked the conference with a proposal that somehow bridged the divide between those who advocated for massive and rapid evangelization of the world and those who wished to reform the world by engaging with social justice. After cross-referencing data from the world's "unreached" with the gospel and the "poorest of the poor," he was astonished to see drawn on his computer screen a rectangular strip stretching across Africa, the Middle East, and Asia between approximately 10 and 40 degrees latitude north of the equator, where the majority of Muslims, Hindus, and Buddhists lived.

This "Resistant Belt," as evangelicals saw it, was preventing Christianity from taking over the world. And it was to become the focus of all efforts of the global evangelical movement they had been nurturing. The idea wasn't to liberate its inhabitants from extreme poverty and oppression, as liberals had proposed, but from being "enslaved" by Islam, Hinduism, and Buddhism. US conservative evangelicals and their disciples in Latin America believe they are fighting spiritual battles, and they see poverty, wars, and disasters as caused by evil forces to which the only solution is Evangelism. Bush had created the map for Christian expansion in the twenty-first century. He called it the 10/40 Window.

“This Crusade”

On the morning when God spoke to him for the first time, S. P. Luiz woke up at dawn for his usual devotional and Bible reading, had a quick breakfast at the budget motor inn where he had spent the night, and hit the road again. He had lost count of the days away from home, traveling with three fellow evangelical pastors on a ten-thousand-kilometer-long prayer trip from Brazil’s eastern coast to Colombia. From the window of the rusty pickup truck, he saw Quilombo dos Palmares, where enslaved Muslims, brought from Africa by the Portuguese to work in the plantations and forcibly converted to Christianity, had organized the colony’s first slave rebellion. The itinerary had not been planned. As it is with everything for Luiz, a “born again” Protestant evangelical, God was his guide.

Suddenly, he had a vision of “demons descending from the open sky; huge demons bringing rows upon rows of armament . . . bomb explosions . . . debris and blood, and a great army crossing a portal,” which he attributed to some kind of a curse. Visions had caused him trouble before and distanced him from the church, for those in his religious inner circle believed he had been possessed by evil spirits. *They are back*, Luiz thought, in agony.

Luiz asked the pastor to stop the car. Under the scorching sun, he knelt by the roadside and, holding up his hands, prayed in silence: *God, have mercy on me. If this is not coming from You, please make me stop seeing them.* The group moved to the nearest rest stop. On a big-screen TV inside the local diner, Luiz watched in disbelief as United Airlines Flight 175 crashed into the south tower of the World Trade Center. Then he learned that American Airlines Flight 11 had struck the north tower seventeen minutes earlier. *The vision*, he thought to himself.

In many ways, 9/11 took on apocalyptic significance, and purposefully or not, the White House's immediate response was enveloped in an aura of redemption. In his first address to the nation on the evening of the attacks, President George W. Bush invoked Psalm 23: "Even though I walk through the valley of the shadow of death, I fear no evil, for You are with me." At the Washington National Cathedral's 9/11 memorial service three days later, Bush pledged to "rid the world of evil" as America's duty. "Nothing can separate us from God's love," he assured the audience. "And may He always guide our country."

The president spent the weekend confined with his National Security Council at Camp David and on the phone with foreign leaders to build an international coalition against terrorism. Speaking to journalists back in the White House that Sunday, Bush repeated "evil-doers" five more times and urged Americans to return to work because "this crusade, this war on terrorism, is going to take a while." It was a regretful choice of words.

The term *crusade* immediately sparked an international backlash. President Bush dropped the word and, in the following months, hosted Ramadan dinners, visited mosques, and made public speeches praising Islam as a religion of peace. The president called the terrorists "traitors to their own faith." In his address to a joint session of Congress on September 20, 2001, Bush acknowledged that citizens from eighty nations were killed on 9/11 and thanked people's prayers "in English, Hebrew, and Arabic" from South Korean Christian children gathered outside the US embassy in Seoul to Muslims assembled at a mosque in Cairo.

Between the lines, however, Bush's communication remained highly familiar to his most faithful voters. He referred to the US as a nation awakened and called to defend freedom. Bush summoned "every nation in every region" in the world to make a decision: "Either you are with us, or you are with the terrorists," the president said, paraphrasing Matthew 12:30: "He who is not with Me is against Me."

As the US moved on with plans for intervention in Afghanistan, the US Department of Defense designated the military operation "Infinite Justice," which to Muslims only Allah can provide (in the face of harsh criticism, the campaign was quickly renamed Operation Enduring Freedom).

Then, during his State of the Union Address on January 20, 2002, Bush branded North Korea, Iran, and Iraq the "axis of evil," even though the terrorists responsible for 9/11 came from none of those countries. A little more than a year later, the US began bombing Iraq. When Bob Woodward, whose book *Plan of Attack* is a detailed account of the administration's steps toward Iraq, asked Bush if he had sought advice from his father, who avoided an invasion of Iraq after Saddam Hussein's forces escaped out of Kuwait in 1991, the president responded: "There is a higher father that I appeal to."

Much of the theological framework of the White House communication after the 9/11 attacks is credited to President Bush's chief speechwriter, Michael Gerson, a conservative evangelical Christian and graduate of Wheaton College. "Gerson's words shaped the war on terror as a Biblical battle between good and evil, and helped sell Americans the Iraq War," the *Washington Post* wrote in his obituary.

It could be difficult to separate Bush's overtly religious language from his association with exponents of the Christian Right, such as Billy Graham's son Franklin, who delivered the invocation at Bush's first inauguration and had a close relationship with the president. Graham made headlines post-9/11 by denouncing Islam as a "wicked" and "evil religion." In separate instances, televangelist Pat Robertson said on his *700 Club* television program that Islam was "not a peaceful religion." At the same time, the Moral Majority's Jerry Falwell declared on CBS's *60 Minutes* that "Muhammad was a terrorist," and the Southern Baptist Convention's former president Jerry Vines called the Prophet Muhammad a "demon-possessed pedophile."

Liberal Christian organizations such as the National Council of Churches disagreed. Even some conservative evangelical leaders reacted. The National Association of Evangelicals and the Institute on Religion and Democracy published a three-page "Guideline on Christian-Muslim Dialogue," which called on Christian leaders to tone down their language about Islam. Not that the evangelical leaders unanimously disagreed with Graham's derogatory words on Islam. Many, in fact, avoided personally criticizing Graham and others. But for those involved in Christian missions, inflammatory anti-Islamic remarks could threaten work overseas. As noted by Ted Olsen in *Christianity Today*, "In talking with Muslims, the guidelines say Christians must give testimony to the Gospel of Jesus Christ because it is our duty to do so."

What evangelicals viewed as their duty was in line with President Bush's own understanding of America's duty to the world. As part of Bush's broad security strategy post-9/11, the president promised to make "special efforts to promote freedom of religion and conscience." Bush's faith-based internationalism came as a blessing to US evangelicals involved in missionary work abroad. Freedom of religion abroad meant freedom to evangelize in countries closed to Christian missions, mostly Muslim-majority nations. But it greatly worried foreign relations experts. "I agree that there is evil," Carol Hamrin, senior associate of the Christian think tank Institute for Global Engagement, told *Christianity Today*. "But my point is practical: if we operate on the mindset that we are right and they are wrong, we lose the complexities. People need to sense you are willing to accept them if they don't accept your values or ideas. Have we communicated that to the Muslims?"

Since the fall of the Berlin Wall in 1989, the global evangelical movement has increasingly turned its attention from communism to Islam. Between 1990 and 2003, the number of missionaries in Islamic countries quadrupled. "On September Eleven, we felt the painful consequences of largely ignoring the Muslim world. For most of the last five centuries since the Protestant Reformation, the church has done relatively little to bring the Gospel of Christ to the Muslim peoples of the world," Rick Wood, then managing editor of *Mission Frontiers*, wrote two months after the attacks on 9/11. He called believers to take a firm stand for religious freedom. "The civilized world has declared war on terrorism. Now it is up to Christians to tear down the strongholds of Satan that have held the Muslim peoples in bondage for hundreds of years. It's time for us to set these captives free."

Wood's article was a farewell letter. On January 15, 2002, he was leaving his job at *Mission Frontiers* to work with Luis Bush, who in 2001 began working on a global survey of Christian leaders titled "Evangelizing Our World Inquiry," co-sponsored by the Lausanne Movement, to serve as a blueprint for world evangelization in the twenty-first century.

In the years since he introduced the 10/40 Window, Bush had founded and led several other initiatives; traveled to Brazil, Venezuela, Chile, Bolivia, Honduras, Guatemala, Mexico, and Hispanic churches in the US; and channeled support and funding to Latin American churches. He also founded the AD2000 Movement, calling for "a church for every people and the gospel for every person" before the end of the millennium. It was described as "the largest, most pervasive global evangelical network ever to exist." But, having survived the turn of the new millennium and the End Times prophecies that emerged with it, global Evangelists began questioning: "Now what?"

When anti-Islam rhetoric surged after 9/11, many evangelicals felt that the time had come for a significant push to proselytize to Muslims, who could be questioning the acts of fundamentalist coreligionists in the name of their own faith.

Aspiring missionaries filled US classrooms to learn how to evangelize Muslims. Churches responded to the call from evangelical organizations, sending many missionaries to the borders of Afghanistan, as they waited to enter the country on the trail of American troops. "When radical Islamic terrorists brought down the World Trade Center's Twin Towers," the *Baptist Press* wrote," they didn't realize their actions would also help bring down walls to reaching Muslims with the Gospel."

Hundreds of Americans volunteered with the International Mission Board (IMB) to distribute food and shelter to Iraqis, and to help them "have true freedom in Jesus Christ." The International Bible Society printed thousands upon thousands of a Scripture booklet at forty cents each, funded with donations, and shipped them to Iraq. Kyle Fisk, then the executive administrator of the powerful National Association of Evangelicals, anticipated that Iraq would "become the center for spreading the gospel of Jesus Christ to Iran, Libya, throughout the Middle East." The evangelical Trans World Radio began airing in Arabic and Farsi. "Not for a century has the idea of evangelizing Islam awakened such fervor in conservative Christians," *Time* magazine declared. American missionary zeal and dollars helped "fuel the biggest evangelical foray into the Muslim world" in one hundred years, according to *Mother Jones* magazine.

During Bush's first term in office, US federal funds to faith-based organizations grew dramatically. Tracking this money is challenging, but a yearlong investigation by the *Boston Globe* provides a glimpse of how federal grants were distributed. The team examined 159 FBOs that received over $1.7 billion in USAID prime contracts and agreements from 2001 to 2005. During this period, the percentage of US funds channeled to faith-based groups doubled, with twenty cents of every USAID dollar going to them. Out of 159 prime contracts with FBOs, only two Muslim groups received any grants, with 98 percent of the funds going to Christian groups, even though most of the work was done in majority-Muslim countries.

Most aid groups have signed the International Federation of Red Cross and Red Crescent Societies code of conduct, affirming that "aid will not be used to further a particular political or religious standpoint." But several faith-based organizations have a clear proselytizing agenda. Franklin Graham's Samaritan's Purse has been criticized for a host of violations: holding prayer services before seminars funded by USAID in El Salvador; showing a film about Jesus in Jordan; and giving New Testaments to Gulf War troops to be distributed to locals in Saudi Arabia.

Thousands of Christian workers and missionaries were arriving in the Middle East on the heels of an invading army led by a deeply religious US president, whose most loyal constituency was conservative evangelicals, some of whom were unapologetically anti-Muslim. The Muslim world already viewed America as waging war against Islam, and it was not difficult to anticipate how any attempt to proselytize could be explosive. For Muslims on the ground, the US-led war on terror was nothing short of a crusade.

In November 2002, a thirty-one-year-old nurse's assistant at the Christian and Missionary Alliance prenatal clinic in Sidon, Lebanon, was shot dead by an unknown assailant. Local imams denounced members of the alliance, which was partially funded by Samaritan's Purse, for allegedly proselytizing and handing out Christian material, the *New York Times* reported. A few months earlier, an attempted operation to rescue American missionaries Martin and Gracia Burnham from the Islamic militant group Abu Sayyaf came to a tragic end when Martin was killed and Gracia was wounded.

Then in December of that year, three American missionaries were shot dead at the Jibla Baptist Hospital, owned by the Southern Baptist Convention, in Yemen. The gunman, a Muslim radical, accused his victims of "preaching Christianity in a Muslim country." The hospital had operated in the country for more than thirty-five years, underscoring the changes in safety conditions for missionaries on the ground. "This is not a conflict between religions but a conflict between God and Satan, between good and evil," Jack Graham (no relation to Billy and Franklin), then president of the Southern Baptist Convention, told the *New York Times*.

Calls for limiting the sending of missionaries and forbidding proselytizing began to grow, with advocates arguing that the presence of American missionaries jeopardized the work of humanitarian organizations and put American soldiers at higher risk.

At a meeting in Seoul, South Korea, in May 2003, Luis Bush shared preliminary findings of his World Inquiry. The mission strategist found that there was a growing concern with the presence of American missionaries in the field; in Bush's words, "a need that missionaries from other countries are often better able to fill." The US role in missions was changing to "empowering nationals." After consulting nearly seven thousand evangelical Christian leaders from eight hundred cities around the world, most of them in Latin America, Africa, and Asia, Bush concluded: "God is calling His servants to act as catalysts in mobilizing the whole body of Christ to bless the nations through the transformation of people, churches, and culture."

The question wasn't whether or not to continue sending missionaries to conflicted zones hostile to them, but whom to send. "Somebody is going to have to risk their life to bring the Gospel to the Yemenites," American evangelist Timothy Tennent, then director of missions programs at Gordon-Conwell, told the *Christian Science Monitor*. "The question is, who should it be?" The story found that missionaries adjusted to risks in Arab lands by steering clear of Muslim nations and training Latinos to go instead. "Latinos, Filipinos, and other non-Western Christians are thus increasingly staffing the front lines of the world's most dangerous mission fields," the article reads.

Bush presented the complete findings of his inquiry at the 2004 Forum on World Evangelization in Thailand, hosted by the Lausanne Committee. "One more very powerful reason for activating the whole missions movement is because the 'Western face' is no longer as welcome as it once was. Our non-Western colleagues come free from the 'arrogance and triumphalism' associated with Western Christianity. Particularly working in hostile Islamic States, the Western presence brings too much baggage," read a conference paper. "Today, it is more acceptable to have a Latin American, African, or Asian missionary in Muslim countries."

The safety of missionaries wasn't the only or even the primary concern among US Evangelists. They worried about how effective American missionaries could be in places with high anti-Western convictions. "After 9/11, it makes it very unlikely a

Muslim is going to be able to hear the Gospel from an American," Tennent said. "If we can send a Brazilian or a Russian to do it more effectively, that's all the better."

"So, suddenly, you had all these internationals, who don't carry the baggage of the colonial era or of the West toward the Muslim world, and they shared the culture and skin color. They didn't represent a threat to anybody, and they were there, ready for the higher calling of God," Luis Bush told me at an evangelical summit in Indonesia years later. It was as if God had been preparing Latin Americans precisely for that moment.

Vinci Barros had been S. P. Luiz's pastor for some fifteen years when Luiz shared his 9/11 "vision from God." Raised poor by a single working mother, Barros had been expelled from school in his teens, and even sentenced to a few months in prison for drug possession. He was first attracted to the church when a group of missionaries from the United States staged a play on the life and death of his idol, Jimi Hendrix. The American missionaries were members of the Jesus People Movement, a conservative alternative to the counterculture of the 1960s. Tens of thousands of young Christians gathered in Dallas for the movement's Expo '72, the largest religious camp ever to take place in the US up to that time. Over 150,000 people showed up on the last night for an eight-hour Jesus rock concert featuring Johnny Cash. Billy Graham called it "religious Woodstock."

In Brazil, the movement introduced Christian rock to the masses and used theater to reach street children and troubled youth. Barros converted to evangelical Christianity and started ministering among drug addicts, prostitutes, gamblers, and burglars. He attended theological training at the Wesleyan

Seminary in Nilópolis, Rio de Janeiro. He became a minister of the church, where he met his wife, Samia, the daughter of a Wesleyan pastor ministering in the United States.

Barros's street ministry eventually led him to be expelled from the denomination for being "unorthodox." A group of fellow churchgoers followed him, and Barros started his own house church. He began getting involved with missions. As a minister of the Wesleyan Methodist Church in Rio, Barros had met the California-born James Robert Stier, or Jimy, then a Youth With A Mission (YWAM) missionary to South America. Jimy and his wife, Pamela, moved from Colombia to Brazil in 1975 to start a YWAM base in Contagem, Minas Gerais. From there, YWAM spread throughout the country. "Jimy was very charismatic and got me interested in missions and the persecuted church," Barros said.

In 1977, Operation Mobilization, a Christian missionary organization started by a young American missionary during a summer outreach in Mexico, purchased the ship *Doulos* (Greek for "servant") and, two years later, began recruiting young Brazilians to serve on board. Barros enthusiastically joined. By the time *Doulos* left Latin America in June 1983, after five years in and out of the region, it had welcomed over 4.1 million visitors and distributed over four hundred thousand copies of Christian literature. In October of that year, Barros attended the Brazilian Congress of Evangelization, the first national gathering of the Lausanne Movement. It was held in Belo Horizonte, Brazil's third largest metropolitan area, where an enthusiastic crowd of believers filled an entire soccer stadium. There, delegates pledged their allegiance to the Lausanne Covenant and their adherence to the global missions movement under the auspices of the Lausanne Commission for World Evangelization.

Religious leaders like Barros see the conservative Brazilian Congress as a turning point for the evangelical church in Latin America. In 1987, Luis Bush and other conservative leaders in the subcontinent founded COMIBAM, the Ibero-American Missions Cooperation. It proved to be Latin America's most important mission network. Bertuzzi, the pastor on board the *Doulos*, later became the organization's executive director, and Barros joined the flocks with several other young evangelical missions enthusiasts who came out of *Doulos*.

Soon after, Barros co-founded the Conselho Ide às Nações ("Go to the Nations Council") with other emerging leaders from Brazil, a national movement aimed at awakening the Brazilian church to national and world missions. His house-church had grown organically into a network of cells across Brazil and beyond, as members moved to other parts of the country and abroad. The church didn't commission any missionaries yet at that time, but Barros had been seriously thinking about and praying for it.

"The 10/40 Window influenced pretty much every evangelical missionary. It was a turning point for missions. We all got impacted by that view," Barros told me. "Then came 9/11 and its spiritual impact. It was fundamental. It opened the doors into Afghanistan, thanks to the United States. But Americans were seen with suspicion around the world, so they could not go because of the imperialistic and oppressive image that the country had."

As the field became too dangerous for American missionaries, Barros said, US evangelicals appealed to a cohort of like-minded leaders in the South. This time, it wasn't a call from God, but from America. "The US call to the Church in Brazil was strong, because we are a neutral country. And because of our soccer and music, Brazilians are welcome and loved everywhere." Barros also felt that missions leaders in Brazil were in debt to Americans. "The US has always been the country funding [missions]. It paved the way for Christian missions and NGOs to reach Afghanistan and other places. We all benefited from it." So, Barros began considering sending his own disciples into perilous Muslim fields.

At Barros's invitation, S. P. Luiz had quit his job as a construction manager and moved, with his wife, Gis, and his children, to lead a newly formed church cell with some thirty disciples in São Luís do Maranhão. The island lies off the northeast coast of Brazil, in the Atlantic, and Luiz liked to walk alone on the beach in the dead of night, praying in silence. One night, he heard a voice. "God spoke to me as clearly as you are talking to me now," he said when we first met, staring at me as if expecting my skeptical reaction. "'I will take you across the seas. This land I am showing you. . . . Go there, and once there, I will give you signs.'" Beyond the ocean, high in the starry sky of São Luís do Maranhão, "the world map opened like an LED TV, and the 10/40 Window appeared." Then, a country popped up. It was Afghanistan.

"God showed me Afghanistan, and I saw that it was at the heart of the 10/40 Window, a very strategic place that bordered six countries. I had heard about the window, but it was something very far away," Luiz told me. "I had no idea where Afghanistan was."

"Forget about it," Gis snapped when he told her about his vision. Then, the couple received a call from Barros, who said he had been praying to God about sending missionaries to Afghanistan, so Luiz told him about his vision. "Oh, so that is it," Barros reacted. Luiz had barely ventured outside Brazil, and neither had Gis or anyone else in the family. But, soon after, the couple and their two children moved as undercover missionaries to Afghanistan.

Among the Believers

Luiz and Gis first landed in Afghanistan in October 2003 for a weeklong scouting trip. They flew from São Luís do Maranhão to São Paulo, in Brazil, to Frankfurt, in Germany, to Baku, in Azerbaijan, and from there on a decrepit mid-1960s Tupolev long retired from the former Soviet fleet but still in operation in less popular routes. Except for the mosquitoes flying along with the passengers, the last of the four legs went smoothly, and the couple finally arrived at Kabul International Airport.

The airport was a junkyard of wrecked tanks and military planes left to deteriorate after the Soviet Red Army ended its ten-year occupation of Afghanistan and withdrew from the country in early 1989. They sat alongside twisted metal and debris from the Taliban Air Force aircraft bombed out in the earlier days of the US-led campaign after 9/11. A crush of people waited on the dirt, gravel, and pothole terrain outside. Bearded traders carrying bundles of cash hoped to exchange afghanis for US dollars. Street children dug through the garbage; some offered cigarettes and matches, others tried unsuccessfully to shine off the thin layer of sand that covered visitors' shoes. Elderly, handicapped men pleaded for alms, while women begged from under their burqas. "It was ugly, ugly, ugly," Luiz recalled. "We started crying."

Luiz and Gis believed they were witnessing the suffering mankind would endure once the End Times approached, as described in the Book of Revelations. They were convinced that the suffering of Afghans had a reason: the lack of saving faith in Jesus. While the reality on the ground was shocking, the people looked somehow familiar. Their faces and garments resembled those the couple had seen in photographs of the "unreached people groups" that circulated in Christian magazines and newsletters.

Afghanistan lies at the heart of the 10/40 Window. To evangelicals, the country was the ultimate battleground in the spiritual wars between Christianity and the "evil" forces of communist atheism, in which God and the capitalist West were victorious, and between Christianity and the new threat of Islamic extremism in the twentieth-first century. According to the list put together by the Joshua Project, a research initiative started within Luis Bush's AD2000 Movement, Afghanistan has one of the world's largest populations of "unreached" people. The country boasts a patchwork of ethnic groups—Pashtuns, Tajiks, Hazaras, Uzbeks, Turkmen, Balochis, and several other minorities, further divided into a multitude of subethnic-linguistic groups, tribes, and clans. Various conquerors have trespassed on Afghan territory, dating back to Alexander the Great. However, as the British, the Russians, and the Americans would painfully learn, none of the invaders held these lands for long.

Five of Barros's brethren from different parts of Brazil, who had been considering becoming missionaries, had joined Luiz and Gis in the final leg of the journey. A young woman serving with the Christian charity World in Need (WIN) welcomed them. A trusted Afghan driver with a white van drove the group to WIN's office in Taimani, just eight kilometers away, in northwestern Kabul. Ron George, the founder of WIN, greeted the group and shared with them relevant information about cultural sensitivities, the security situation, and mandatory safety measures and rules. None in the group spoke English, and the Brazilian host translated George's words to Portuguese. But nobody seemed to be listening, anyway. "Our first impression of Afghanistan was of shock. It was awful, because Brazilians had never seen war or the destruction caused by a war." The group prayed.

Luiz and Gis stayed that night with a missionary couple from Argentina. After years living in Afghanistan, the couple told Luiz, they had only made a handful of converts.

The next morning, the Afghan driver came to pick Luiz and Gis up, and they joined the other Brazilian church fellows in the white van. During this first weeklong stay in Afghanistan, the group served with the Christian humanitarian aid organization Shelter Now International. The NGO was founded by Arizona-born Douglas Layton and a group of self-described "committed Christians" to assist Afghan refugees fleeing across the border into Pakistan after the Soviet invasion in 1979. Layton later moved on to work in the semi-autonomous region of Kurdistan in northern Iraq.

Shelter Now came to the world's attention in August 2001, just weeks before 9/11. Its new director, Georg Taubmann, and seven other Westerners, including Americans Dayna Curry and Heather Mercer of the Antioch Church in Waco, Texas, as well as sixteen Afghans, were arrested by the Taliban for showing a film about Jesus to an Afghan family. When the American military campaign began on October 7, the extremists freed the Afghans and retreated toward Kandahar, the Taliban's birthplace, taking the foreigners with them. The hostages were eventually rescued by anti-Taliban fighters. A few months after being freed, Taubmann returned to Afghanistan and resumed his ministry with Shelter Now. "We are here to help Afghan people. We are known to be Christians, probably now even more than before. We still have the same rules. When people ask us about our faith, and of course many do, we talk with them about it," he told *Christianity Today*. To most missionaries I encountered in Afghanistan and elsewhere in the Muslim world, that was not proselytizing. Taubmann added, "Well, if you have friends and they want to see a film about the life of Jesus, and Jesus is one of the most respected prophets, what big crime is that?"

Taubmann reinstated Shelter Now's project to rebuild several villages in the Shamali Plain that had been devastated by the Taliban. Hundreds of thousands of refugees were returning to their homeland only to find their houses in ruins or completely destroyed. The villages had no electricity and no running water. The transitional government was struggling to provide security, and warlords fought to secure territory in post-Taliban Afghanistan. But there was hope.

Located 1,700 meters above sea level, the mountain village had fresher air and more pleasant temperatures than in the capital. In the once-deserted ancient village, Afghan returnees deepened dry wells, cleaned out ancient canals, and plowed the land where they planned to plant acacia, apricot, plum, and peach trees, if the weather allowed. Bee colonies gave them a hand, and some villagers made wooden hives to produce honey. Others worked at producing roof beams and housing components in a small concrete factory established by Shelter Now.

Next to the factory, Shelter Now ran a school. Gis spent the day picking lice from the girls' tangled, dusty hair, then washing and combing them. Outside, Luiz helped distribute donated clothes that had just arrived. When they finished the work, he improvised a soccer ball made of socks and began playing. Soon, dozens of little boys surged onto the field like ants coming out of an anthill. "I counted some one hundred kids," Luiz said.

Many Afghan children had disabilities caused by Soviet-era land mines, the brutal civil war that followed, or the lack of vaccination. Most houses in Afghanistan had no running water or sanitation, and families relied on the hammams, or public bathhouses, where boys covered in coal dust fueled the fire that warmed the water. Food was bought daily because there were no refrigerators.

That night, Luiz and Gis had trouble falling asleep. The two kneeled on the bedroom floor. "We cried and prayed. We asked the Lord to show us what He wanted us to see there because we could only see the losses. We asked God to confirm His call in our hearts. We asked Him to bring us peace and certainty," Gis wrote in her journal. "We are in no man's land." Deep in their hearts, Luiz and Gis were unsure and frightened by the prospect of moving to Afghanistan, and Luiz's trust in the visions that had led him to the war-torn country was sometimes shaken. Sharing such feelings with church fellows could be seen as a lack of faith, but they privately confessed their fears and doubts to each other and prayed for some kind of divine confirmation. "I said: Lord, open our eyes, for we are blind," Gis recalled, paraphrasing Isaiah 35:5. "I was desperate. Kabul was all destroyed, I had never seen anything like that before, and it greatly impacted me. I couldn't see how we could live with our children here."

Then, Gis had a dream: "God gave me glasses and told me that I'd see through Jesus's eyes," she recalled. To Gis, that meant she would no longer see the misery, the disorder, or the destruction all around but what was "in people's hearts." In the morning before dawn, Luiz walked to the guesthouse's backyard and knelt outside in prayer. He had barely closed his eyes all night and instead broke down weeping, then watched in amusement as the tears touched the earthen floor. "I remembered something that God told me when I had that vision: Your tears will touch the land, and I will transform this nation," he recalled years later. "I know it sounds pretentious, but that is what God told me."

In the afternoon that day, heavy clouds darkened the sky above the Shomali Plains. Through an interpreter, Luiz asked an Afghan villager if it would rain. "He said, 'No way! It hasn't rained here for seven years since the Taliban took power.' But then I walked just fifty meters and . . . it rained! It rained a lot. There were sections of the road that were flooded on the way back. That was tremendous!" he recalled. To Luiz and Gis, that was no coincidence. "It is Jesuscidence," Luiz said with a laugh.

On Friday, the Afghan day of rest, Luiz and Gis were staying with the Argentinian missionary couple when a man knocked at the door. The old, fragile Afghan villager, with facial bones visible under his sun-cracked skin, said he came from the mountains and had been diagnosed with leukemia. Someone had told him that there was a doctor in the house, and he hoped for a miracle. The Brazilian doctor in the group offered to examine the man, and Luiz asked if they could pray for him. "Jesus can heal you," Luiz said, holding the man's hands. He agreed. So the South American missionaries extended their arms upward, hands held above the man's head, and prayed for his cure in Portuguese while the Argentinian pastor translated their words to Dari. When the prayer ended, Luiz held the man tightly in a hug. "He was filled with the [Holy] Spirit and collapsed in Sandro's arms," Gis wrote in another letter to her family. Luiz told him about "the love of Jesus Christ," and the man promised to return.

Luiz and Gis believed the encounter with the Afghan villager was the last of three "divine signs" so the couple would know that moving to Afghanistan was indeed God's call, though to Gis it felt more like a curse. "God, this cannot be true! It's impossible!" she remembers thinking, but only to herself so as not to influence Luiz's decision on whether or not the family should move to Afghanistan. "As the days passed, we got more and more desperate," she wrote in her journal. "We asked God: how will we live with our children here?"

In one of the first letters to her family in Brazil, Gis wrote: "I wanted a miracle. God gave me many. He gave me spiritual glasses to see that those people are loved by Him, but are in the darkness. We asked the Lord to show us what He wanted. He showed us a white field for harvesting, where God wants us to announce His Kingdom! I am not crazy to go to such a place, if not sent by the Lord. But how will they hear without someone preaching to them? And how will they preach unless they are sent?" she said. Looking back, Gis said, "I knew there was no turning back."

The couple returned to Brazil to say goodbye to family and friends and to pick up their children. The grandparents pleaded with the couple to leave the boys behind. "I felt their pain in my heart. The idea of having us become missionaries in Afghanistan was daunting to them. Just talking about going abroad was horrible," Gis told me. "The boys were very attached to my mother-in-law, and she didn't even know where Afghanistan was. Most people in Brazil didn't. But they knew that nothing would hold us back anymore." Luiz's mother "cried in pain" when she learned about the couple's plans. Gis's mother fell sick. She started having frequent panic attacks that triggered an enduring, severe depression, and she could no longer be left alone. She would spend days "trapped in bed, scared like a cornered animal, crying endlessly." As the time to move away approached, a deep feeling of loss and grief took over them all. The entire church united to pray for the family.

"At that time, people began having dreams," Luiz said. And these dreams were all interpreted like signs and messages from God, giving the family comfort and direction. "It all really happened, just as they had seen in dreams." Again, Luiz and Gis quit their jobs—his as a pastor and hers as a primary school teacher. The couple left their home in São Luís do Maranhão with one suitcase each, carrying only personal belongings and leaving all the furniture and appliances for the pastor who would replace Luiz. They sold an old car and air-conditioning unit to help pay for four tickets to Afghanistan, as the church donations were insufficient.

The family spent a period in Scotland learning English. There they lived rent-free in a pastoral house of the Baptist Church in Edinburgh. Luiz took a part-time job cleaning bathrooms at a telecom company for £600 a month while Gis took care of the children. A good soul offered to pay the gas bill after visiting the family one night and finding them freezing. Other church members helped out by giving them things like used pots and cutlery. "We went through some difficult times," Gis said. "But God was moving us. And He will provide if He wants us to go to a certain place." In October 2005, the family finally moved to Kabul, carrying a bundle of clothes, a recipe book, a second-hand acoustic guitar, and a donated Nintendo for the boys, then seven and twelve. Afghanistan was home now.

When I first visited the family, Gis was cooking *tutu de feijão*, a Brazilian bean dish, on a wood-fired oven at their home in the Kabul neighborhood of Kart-e-Char. It was April 2011, and Afghanistan was in flames. The snow had melted on the mountains, clearing the roads for the Taliban to start their yearly spring offensive. That meant the fighting season was open. In a statement, the Taliban promised to target "the invading Americans and their foreign allies and internal supports." There were about forty insurgent attacks across the country daily, a sharp increase from the previous year. With 150,000 troops on the ground, the American military presence in Afghanistan was at its highest, as was the anti-American sentiment.

Days earlier, radical pastor Terry Jones had presided over a mock trial of the Koran in front of his church, the Dove World Outreach Center, in Gainesville, Florida, and then set a copy of the Islamic scriptures on fire. Jones was condemned by high-profile evangelicals in the US. He was later arrested on charges of unlawful conveyance of fuel for carrying a barbecue grill filled with 2,998 kerosene-soaked Korans, one for every victim of the 9/11 terrorist attacks, which he intended to burn. But that did not prevent a video of the mock trial of the Koran from going viral. The image sparked protests across the Muslim world, including in several provinces in Afghanistan. In Mazar-i-Sharif, home to another Brazilian missionary serving with the YWAM, an enraged mob walked to the local headquarters of the United Nations Assistance Mission and killed seven foreigners, then set the compound alight. It remains the deadliest attack on the UN in nearly two decades. "Death to America!" they shouted.

Luiz was a big man with Scandinavian features, thanks to his Swedish great-grandmother. He had a full head of thick hazel hair, a patchy beard, and deep blue-green eyes. If it weren't for his six foot, three inches and 264 pounds, some might even say that he resembled Jesus (or at least Western depictions of Him). In the streets of Kabul, that meant he was an easy target. Luiz didn't seem to worry. When I arrived, he greeted me with a hug, to the startled looks of passersby. Unlike in Latin America, where even strangers might greet each other with a warm hug and cheek kisses, physical contact between men and women is nowhere to be seen on the streets of Afghanistan. To Luiz, the public demonstration of affection had a higher purpose: to display "the love of Christ." I doubted Afghans saw it that way.

Kart-e-Char is opposite the highly secured embassies and compounds of Kart-e-Say, Kabul's foreign enclave. Houses had no numbers, so we agreed to meet at a corner of the main road, just a few blocks from where thirty-four-year-old Gayle

Williams, an aid worker born in Zimbabwe, had been gunned down in broad daylight on her way to work in Kabul. Williams was a staff member of a Christian faith-based organization named Serve Afghanistan. The Taliban claimed responsibility for the killing and accused Serve of preaching Christianity. I wondered if Luiz wasn't scared. "Did you forget? He brought me here," he said. How about Gayle? I asked. "Well, we never know what plans God had for her."

As we walked toward the house, the air smelled of open sewage, kabuli pulao (a traditional Afghan rice dish), and Brazilian black beans. Gis came to greet me. She was delicate-featured and looked smaller when standing next to Luiz, but she was not short of presence. One needed just a few seconds to understand she was the flock's leader, hosting the guests, attending the children, preparing the food while guiding those helping bring the dishes from the kitchen with a commanding but affable voice, and ensuring everyone felt at home. She had fair skin, brown eyes, and shoulder-length hair, just recently dyed red by her husband. "Isn't she beautiful?" Luiz asked me. Both were highly affectionate to each other, the kids, and visitors.

The family had electricity only for about two hours a day, and the wood-fired stove helped heat the living room. A long ten-seat table placed by the window faced a dormant garden covered by small piles of snow. Around the table, the atmosphere was warm, and the mood was festive. They had friends coming all the time, and there was always the need to "add water to the cooking beans," as Brazilians say cheerfully when they have more mouths to feed than expected. Their frequent guests were mostly missionaries from Brazil, South Africa, Nigeria, China, Romania, and South Korea. The only North

American in Luiz's evangelical circle in Afghanistan was a man married to a Chinese missionary. Across the house's backyard was a one-bedroom shed they rented to Christian workers on short-term missions to help pay the bills. A Filipino had just left, and now the room was occupied by a senior missionary from New Zealand and a stray dog she had rescued from Kabul's freezing streets. On winter nights, dogs bark incessantly; when there is silence people here worry, for it is not rare to find frozen carcasses outdoors in the morning.

The family was also hosting a single Brazilian woman, a member of Barros's church who was considering becoming a missionary to Muslims. She and the New Zealander joined us at the table. Soon, another Brazilian couple arrived with their two boys for lunch. They had moved to Afghanistan in 2009 to help Luiz's then growing underground ministry. This family had been on the road in the Muslim world since 2001, under the auspices of Jovens Com Uma Missão, the Brazilian branch of Youth With A Mission. They had lived in Lebanon, Cyprus, Egypt, and Syria. During a mission trip to Iraq in May 2003, just a few weeks after Saddam Hussein's statue was toppled in Baghdad, a bomb exploded close to the bus the family traveled in. The mother, pregnant with the couple's third child, was injured and rushed to a nearby Catholic mission hospital. But the doctors couldn't save the baby. A nurse asked the father if he wished to see the fetus. He agreed. Holding it up, he offered his unborn son to God "in sacrifice for saving the Muslim peoples."

All the missionaries sitting around the table had stories of epic adventures, unimaginable risks, severe threats and attacks they had either suffered or witnessed, and a seemingly unbroken faith. Luiz and Gis recalled an attack by suicide bombers against a bus carrying young Afghan soldiers a few blocks away on Darul Aman Road. The explosion was so intense that it had broken the windows by which we were now sitting. On another occasion, Luiz had just left the glassy Safi Landmark Hotel in Kabul's foreigner quarters, after a quick stop for an expresso at the coffee shop on the ground floor, when eight suicide bombers stormed the building, killing the guards at the front doors and detonating explosives almost simultaneously to cause maximum impact. Luiz remembers feeling a sudden intense pressure, followed by the loud noise of the explosions.

The conversation continued for hours over strong Brazilian coffee and dessert—a bowl of doce de leite, a fudgelike Latin American pudding I had brought from Brazil. Luiz recalled how he almost got in trouble twice when working for the Western Christian faith-based organization he first served with in Afghanistan. He had just arrived in the country, and a South Korean coworker asked him for help bringing donations from abroad kept in a container at Kabul International Airport's storage facilities. It turned out that the container was packed with Bibles in the local languages. Kabul policemen and checkpoints were on every corner, and one needed to be out of one's mind to cross the Afghan capital carrying such a massive amount of Christian material. So the missionaries made multiple trips to and from the airport. On one of the last trips, the car suddenly died at a traffic light. There was a checkpoint of the Afghan police just a few meters away, and a car stalled in the middle of the street at night in Kabul would undoubtedly draw the officers' attention. Luiz exited the car and shouted: "In the name of Jesus, move!" As he recalls, the engine restarted, which he interpreted as a miracle. "From then on, all traffic lights were green for us," he told me proudly, adding a Portuguese saying he often used to express what he believed to be "God's provision": *É desse jeito!* ("That's how it is!")

The Christian material was distributed among international missionaries. Luiz and Gis hid them in the (then vacant) annex apartment across their backyard. They called it "the cat's house." The volume was such that the pile rose from the bathtub to the ceiling. The bathroom had been built against a fragile mud wall shared with a neighbor, and one afternoon, the wall collapsed. Nasir, the chowkidar (it translates as "gatekeeper"), saw the boxes amid the ruined wall and rushed to warn Luiz. Handwritten notes like "Bibles in Dari" and "New Testament in Pashto" identified the boxes. Nasir couldn't read, and Luiz had never directly spoken with him about Christianity or his higher purpose in Afghanistan. Still, Nasir's terrified expression suggested the poor man knew what they were.

The second incident happened in 2006 when anti-American riots broke across Kabul after a deadly traffic accident caused by a United States military convoy. Luiz was at the Christian NGO's headquarters with six Afghan staff when angry crowds rampaged through the streets, burning and looting foreign offices. Employees and volunteers were ordered not to leave the building, and rushed to conceal anything that could raise suspicion. Rioters were climbing the walls of the building when an Afghan Army tank turned the corner and dispersed them.

Gis was at home alone when gunshots broke out. She saw smoke clouds rising from a nearby fast-food restaurant the rioters set on fire. Neighbors came and offered to hide her while the chowkidar rushed to pick up the children at school, though they could only go home after the situation was under control.

By the end of the day, at least fourteen people were dead and more than ninety injured in the bloodiest day at the capital since the fall of the Taliban.

Luiz soon quit working with the NGO, but for a different reason. He believed the Western missionaries were making the same mistakes as their predecessors in the colonial era, by bringing aid and Christian textbooks but not truly connecting with the local people. "In Brazil, we would go out and evangelize on the streets. We can't do this here. We need to connect with people and become friends. But they are too scared to walk on the streets. They don't go to the market, they don't talk to people, they don't relate to Afghans like we do."

On a letter to the church in Brazil in late 2006, Luiz wrote: "We need to stop being a team and start being a church . . . and be together outside those meetings." The meetings Luiz referred to were weekly worship services for foreign employees and Afghans converted to Christianity held secretly in the basement of a building rented by the NGO. "Most Afghans can't read, and Western missionaries are all about translating [Christian] tracts and shoving them down their throats. They listened to endless sermons that didn't make sense to them. Afghans sit on the floor. Still, the services were all about getting up, sitting down, in disregard of the local tradition," Luiz complained. "That simply doesn't work here."

The weekly worship, he said, wasn't mandatory but was held during office hours, and Luiz suspected that the Afghan staff understood it as part of the job. He began questioning if they were even real converts. "The Afghans say they are Christians and that's it, they become a number added to the reports that missionaries have to send to their offices and funders in the US and Europe. . . . And, oh, people in the West love reports! But are these new converts really being saved? No. They were there for the job and aid," Luiz said. These organizations were "just buying new Christians," he believed. "We saw these, you know, corporate-like Christian organizations that would inflate the number of converts because they'd get more funding," Luiz said. "This is a land of missionaries and mercenaries." (A "new-born" Afghan who used to participate in the weekly worship and shared Luiz's views later told me that it initially gathered more than one hundred believers, both locals and internationals, but this number would decrease sharply in the following years, as security worsened.)

Afghanistan doesn't recognize Christians. Officially, they do not exist. No religion other than Islam can have a house of worship or be registered. Converting out of Islam makes one an outlaw, and most converts hide their faith even from their parents as it could bring dishonor to the family, not rarely leading relatives to seek "justice" with their own hands. Many continue attending services at a local mosque, so as not to raise suspicion.

The US-backed Afghan Constitution, ratified by President Hamid Karzai on January 26, 2004, acknowledged that followers of all religions were "free to exercise their faith and perform their religious rites." But it also stated that Islam was the religion of the Islamic Republic of Afghanistan, and no law could be contrary to its beliefs and provisions. The only church in the country was a Catholic chapel inside the compound of the Italian embassy, a particular concession to Italy for having been the first country to recognize the independence of Afghanistan in 1919. Only foreigners were allowed in. Afghan converts attended services and Bible classes, if they did, secretly held at offices and homes of foreign missionaries.

Luiz also felt at odds with the NGO when an Afghan convert shared with the group that his father was unemployed and the family struggled to survive. A former police officer during the Soviet-backed regime in Afghanistan, Hussain had fled with his wife and children to Pakistan when the civil war broke out, and stayed there through the subsequent Taliban regime. They lived for almost ten years in a tent at a refugee camp near the border, where Hussain converted to Christianity, and had just recently returned home to Kabul, though they had no home to return to. "They were a big family, his son was visibly hungry, and they would have us pray for hours to him. But just praying is not always the answer. Why am I going to ask God to do something that I can do myself?" Luiz told me. So, at the end of the church service, he approached the young Afghan and said, "Tell your father that he has a job."

Luiz didn't really need an employee, but he was eager to connect with Afghans and saw this as an opportunity. When Hussain came to talk to him about the job, Luiz showed him the one-bedroom shed in the backyard, and said: "This is your room. You can stay here for as long as you need." (Hussain cried when narrating the same episode to me when we met the next year.) "Then we began praying for him to get a better job," Luiz said, jokingly. "But we wouldn't let the family starve until that happened." Four days later, Hussain was hired as WIN's supervisor in Afghanistan, but the two developed a long-lasting friendship. For security reasons, the NGO that Luiz served with at the

time wouldn't allow him to personally relate to locals outside
the office, so he left.

Luiz had been thinking about starting his own business in Afghanistan. In missionary circles, the approach is called *tent-making*, a reference to the Apostle Paul's occupation during his self-supported travel to evangelize and minister. As another Brazilian missionary in Kabul summarized it, in countries closed to Christian workers missionaries can be "job takers, job makers, or job fakers." The trouble lies with the latter, "because they put the entire missionary community at risk." On the other hand, job takers are real professionals who have real jobs. They might proselytize, but most often do it during their off-duty hours, and coworkers might not know their missionary purposes. Job makers, too, run real businesses and create real jobs. Luiz chose the latter. In 2007, he opened a pizza-delivery business in Kabul.

I wondered how anyone could believe that a Latin American had moved from Brazil to a distant, war-torn Afghanistan with a wife and two kids to sell pizza. But Luiz and Gis felt it was a good idea, given the massive presence of foreigners in Kabul; except that Luiz didn't know how to cook pizza. He hired three Afghan Christians—a student of the University of Kabul converted by Filipino missionaries, a young man from Ghazni Province who had escaped persecution for being a Christian and lived with other converts in a guesthouse owned by a Nigerian pastor, and Hussain's youngest son. The trio helped him build a proper, though improvised, oven in the backyard of the family's house, and began cooking.

Expatriates became frequent customers. The company grew even more quickly thanks to a contract with the ISK to supply the international school his children attended with mini-pizzas, bread rolls—and later, more healthy options.

A $9.6 million USAID grant in 2005 had allowed the school to expand. Most ISK teachers lived in the tightly secured school compound for security reasons. Guns, bodyguards, armored vehicles, and daily security restrictions were part of the routine. Each building had bunkers on the rooftop, with emergency supplies of food, water, toilet paper, sleeping bags, and candles. The team carried out insurgent drills to prepare the staff and the students for a potential invasion or rocket attack, in which case they were instructed to wait inside the bunker until a SWAT team arrived to rescue them.

Luiz and Gis's two sons went to the ISK under scholarships that covered half of the school fee (the other half, some $660, was paid with a monthly donation from a Scottish Baptist and friend). The ISK was exempt from the national laws regarding Islamic education, so they were free to provide instruction to Christian children; it was the only school in Afghanistan that mixed local and expat children. Most of the boys' classmates were children of foreign diplomats, United Nations staff, aid workers, and missionaries, but also high-ranking Afghan officials and warlords. "In my class, I study with the sons of an opium baron, a cabinet member, a governor . . ." the older boy said, with a shy laugh.

The brothers' closest friends were Jean-Pierre and Rhodé, the children of South African missionaries Werner and Hannelie Groenewald. Werner had learned about the 10/40 Window while serving as the pastor of the Dutch Reformed Church in Pretoria.

Shortly after 9/11, he went on a short-term mission to the border of Pakistan and Afghanistan. When he returned to Pretoria, Werner took Hannelie to dinner and asked if she would consider moving to Afghanistan. Like Luiz and Gis, they were both thirty-three and well-employed at the time—Werner was a full-time pastor, and Hannelie was a trauma expert in emergency rooms at different hospitals in Pretoria. They lived a "very happy life in South Africa," and their children were just two and four. "I didn't want to go anywhere," Hannelie confessed years later.

It is not that she wasn't a believer. Hannelie was raised by devoted Protestant parents and was an active member of the Christian community in Pretoria. "But I had one foot in the church and another in the secular world," she told me. Nevertheless, Hannelie was brought up to "fear the Lord." "God's call [to Afghanistan] was so clear that I couldn't ignore it." So, in September 2002, the couple traveled to Pakistan's perilous Khyber Pakhtunkhwa province and crossed the high mountains into Afghanistan. Werner grew his beard, and Hannelie wore a burqa. The couple hired an armed guard to accompany them on the most dangerous stretch of the trip: from Peshawar, the capital of Pakistan's semi-autonomous tribal borderlands, to Jalalabad, in Afghanistan. Driving across the Hindu Kush range through the legendary Khyber Pass took sixteen hours. Werner was crying out of emotion. "Just look!" Hannelie recalls him telling her with his eyes fixed on the majestic landscape. "For me, it was an adventure," Hannelie said with a strained smile. "I had no idea what was waiting."

As mothers, Gis and Hannelie shared the same fears and anxieties. Both were born to devoted Protestant parents and raised to fear God's judgment. Both had an unquestioned belief in their husbands' missionary call and offered unrestricted support, even though they were the more "rational" half of the couples, taking care of the house, the children, and everything else that belonged to the earthly world, so their husbands could do "God's work."

Women in Afghanistan, even foreigners, had considerably less freedom than men enjoyed in Afghan society. The strict Taliban dress code was lifted following the US invasion. However, many still wore full blue burqas, and all women were expected to use a conservative garb of loose-fitting pants down to the ankles, knee-length tunics hiding the chest and arms, and the hijab. Gis made life easier by wearing an Arab abaya, a black outer garment covering the whole body, except for her Persian-looking face. As a tall, big-boned, blonde woman, the dress code was more challenging for Hannelie. There were no garments her length, and Werner bought her a secondhand sewing machine so she could make her own clothes. Still, Hannelie rarely left home or walked on the streets without her husband. She felt the piercing stares of Afghan men unsettling, especially toward her daughter, Rhodé.

For the first two years living in Kabul, Hannelie homeschooled her children. Jean-Pierre enrolled at the Hatfield Christian Online School, which used the US-based Accelerated Christian Education program, a "Bible-based K–12 curriculum"; Rhodé took Brainline distance education. It was disastrous, given the unreliable connectivity, constant power cuts, and extended blackouts caused by bomb attacks that destroyed pylons and electric lines bringing power in from Uzbekistan. The children had trouble communicating with the teachers and often missed deadlines while trying to download or upload school material.

Sports and outside activities were restricted. The boys could still play outside, and Werner often took Jean-Pierre cycling. But for girls, that wasn't an option. The lack of movement and exercise prevented Rhodé's muscles from developing adequately, and she suffered from painful scoliosis. Being a Third Culture Kid also meant facing struggles that other children don't, especially in a violent environment such as Afghanistan. Raised in a culture different from that of their parents and their own, TCKs often build a mixed identity that they might not fully relate to. That is especially the case when the cultures influencing their formative years are so different, such as Afghanistan, Brazil, or South Africa.

In the early years in Afghanistan, Hannelie and Gis spent their time caring for the children, helping them cope with restrictions and challenges, doing housework, and hosting many visitors. In separate conversations, the two shared with me how they sometimes felt guilty for involving their children in a dangerous and difficult life, which the boys and the girl had not chosen. But neither had they or their husbands, both women thought, as they believed the two families were just attending God's call. To them, that was the right thing to do.

In Kabul, both families lived on whatever money the church could send—or, as they liked to say, on God's provisions. There were months they could afford dinner out in secret house restaurants run by missionaries. But the budget was often tight. When Luiz got sick, he did not have enough money ($300) to pay for a doctor's appointment or for blood tests and X-rays, available only in the capital's private clinics that served expatriates.

 So, Hannelie saw him for free. She became the doctor of the underground missionary circle in Afghanistan.

In 2007, Hannelie started visiting the notorious Pul-e-Charkhi prison, Afghanistan's largest detention center, to pray with a South African man arrested when he tried to board a plane with nearly six kilograms of heroin. She first sent him a Bible, then began visiting him. Soon other inmates learned that she was a doctor, and prisoners held in dirty cells without proper ventilation or adequate sanitation pleaded to her for care. Soon, Hannelie began attending the prison's guards and ordinary Afghans for free, and sometimes bought them medicine most families couldn't afford.

From the window of her bedroom at the blue house the family first rented, Gis observed children playing amid the ruins of what had once been a theater. One afternoon, she walked there with Nasir, the chowkidar, and found many families living there in tents. The men were out seeking jobs, and Gis asked the women if she could pray for them and the children. She apologized for being unable to pray in their language, and asked them to just close their eyes and listen. She could hear some of them repeating her last word—*Amen*—and took that as a positive sign.

Gis returned to the place several times, bringing mattresses, blankets, and whatever she could donate. Then, she had an idea. She was learning Dari, Afghanistan's most widely spoken language, and needed to practice. Why not invite those women and children home, and teach them English in return? On the first afternoon, only one neighbor came. The next day, there were three. Ten children showed up with their mothers on the third day. Many had nothing to eat, so Gis offered them all a glass of chocolate milk before class. Gis turned the back room of her family home into a carpeted classroom with cushions and a coffee table donated by a South Korean missionary. It was more than students had in some Afghan public schools.

By December 2007, the school had sixty students occupying two rooms in the house. "On Christmas the children prayed and asked Jesus to come into their hearts! They may not even know what they did or the extent of it, but we know that SR [the Lord] heard every prayer and we believe those seeds will sprout," she shared with the church. The students heard "the 'word' every week" at storytime, watched (Christian) cartoons and talked "about our beloved God."

But parents had forbidden a number of children from attending the school out of suspicion that the foreigners were teaching them "Christian things," and others began to gossip about it. "We need wisdom to understand how far we can go," Gis wrote. The Brazilian couple decided to transfer the school to an office across the street, which had been vacated after two American missionaries running English classes for Afghans there were forced to leave the country. Afghan intelligence had paid them a visit, Luiz explained, and the couple vanished that same afternoon. "When something like this happens, you don't take the chance, you just leave, and those who stay behind don't ask any questions."

A German supporter helped with part of the rent while a small church in Brazil promised to cover the costs of electricity and running water. Two Chinese missionaries of the "Back to Jerusalem" movement took over the new pre-school class; a Romanian offered to teach on Saturdays; two Australians developed the Bible-based curriculum. Short-term US missionaries from YWAM were expected to help with whatever else was needed, and others from Iran, Tajikistan, and Uzbekistan raised funds for the tickets and living costs needed for others to join the team. Still, these contributions were not enough and new children arrived daily. Gis launched an "adopt a child" campaign in which donors could sponsor a student for just $15 a month. "We don't have financial conditions to grow," she wrote the church. And that was another reason for starting the pizza-delivery. Ten pizzas sold per day would be enough to cover all of the school's costs, and would free the couple from depending on scattered donations and volunteers.

Letters that Luiz sent the church in Brazil around that time also show financial burdens, growing stress, and family tensions. "Gis is overloaded, and she has the housework to do, and our children need their mother," Luiz wrote. "We cannot win the world and lose our family." It was early 2007, and the first signs of an insurgency against the US-led coalition in Afghanistan had begun to be seen and felt. "There are several fights outside," Luiz wrote. In over seventy letters that Luiz and Gis sent family, friends, and the church in Brazil between 2005 and 2008, the couple's frustrations with the lack of resources and support to handle the risks and challenges they faced in the field are evident. "We are not super men or super women! We need you," Luiz once wrote. Both spoke of feeling lonely and described moments of anguish and great sadness, pessimism and discouragement, sleepless nights and endless crying. In one letter, Gis confessed that the family desired to have a normal life again. "But it's not what God wants," she wrote. To Luiz, the greatest frustration was not being able to evangelize. Then, Luiz met Werner and things began to change.

Like their wives and kids, Luiz and Werner had many things in common. They came from countries with a long history of violence and deep-rooted poverty, so they were not as unfamiliar with Afghanistan's conditions as other foreigners. Both felt they could relate to the suffering of Afghans. Both were products of recent revivals in their countries and were pioneers in foreign transcultural missions of a still-emerging evangelical church in Latin America and Africa. Perhaps more importantly, they were eager to preach the gospel. Luiz had found the perfect partner.

For the first three years in Afghanistan, Werner worked for Global Hope Network International, a secular NGO that aimed at improving the living conditions of people in rural villages and supporting Afghan grassroots organizations. That put Werner in constant contact with ordinary Afghans and tribal leaders in the countryside. He became fluent in Dari (as did Luiz), developed close relationships with some village men, and started to talk to them about his faith. Luiz, too, began visiting remote communities of Pashai people, a subgroup of the ethnic Pashtun. "We visited their villages, gave out Bibles, and taught them about Jesus," Luiz said. It was risky, though at the time the Taliban resurgence was just beginning. But both had sacrificed their family's comfortable life and relative safety in their home countries for a reason. And some Afghans began to respond.

After suffering burnout and spending a sabbatical year with Hannelie and the kids in South Africa, the family returned to Afghanistan in 2008, and Werner decided to leave the NGO. Aid organizations were too scared to hang out with Afghans. Werner wasn't. "This brought us together," Luiz told me. "We are here to do what is possible."

Werner joined a small American-based organization called Partnership in Academic Development (PAD), which offered Afghan young men leadership courses, life management training, and English as a second language. Werner opened PAD's office in Kabul and hired his most trusted converts to work with him. PAD's courses were real and offered to all Afghans. But after hours, the team was dedicated to doing God's work. They translated Christian material into local languages. In the evenings, three times a week, Werner hosted disciples and new converts for Bible studies. He taught them Greek and Hebrew, so the Afghans could interpret the Bible by themselves and become church leaders.

The organization didn't support Werner financially. What it did was secure him a visa and reason to be in the country as part of an organization officially registered with the Afghan government, as required for all foreign enterprises operating in Afghanistan. When Luiz and Gis decided to make the school that she had started at home official, Werner offered to have it affiliated with PAD, on the same terms. The Brazilian missionaries provided him a monthly report on the work done—both secular and religious. At times, Luiz lectured and led prayers to Werner's disciples, and soon the Brazilian missionary began hosting weekly worship services at home for foreign and Afghan converts, which caused a certain discomfort among the international community of Christian workers in Afghanistan. And that, too, brought Luiz and Werner closer.

When one of the last American missionaries stationed in Afghanistan left due to the growing danger, Luiz offered to take the stock of evangelical books and tapes in local languages and dialects that she had to get rid of before leaving. Out of fear, no one would take them.

"No one would work with printed material anymore," Luiz said. "But I just sell pizza. So, I told her: Let me see what I can do with this." Before leaving the country, the US missionary delivered two truckloads of Christian material to Luiz and Gis containing "every material involving Evangelism that you can think of, all in Dari and Pashto," Luiz said. "It was a lot! But I thought to continue her work. If they catch me, I leave. If they kill me, I die. What else can I do? I am here to serve Jesus. I am what I am."

Luiz didn't exactly know what to do with all that material. So he contacted a few key foreign missionaries, and asked if they could set up a meeting with the leaders of the "Afghan church." What Luiz meant by that was a small and scattered group of older Afghan men who had converted from Islam to Christianity while living as refugees in Pakistan in the eighties and nineties and, like Hussain, had returned home after the US invasion. They were trusted and relatively well-versed in the Bible. But, for obvious reasons, they were hard to find. It took months for them to respond during which the Brazilian missionaries kept the material in the rebuilt backyard shed, old trunks, and their basement. Luiz finally reunited the Afghan church. "I need your help," he told them before showing them the hidden material. "They had never seen so many Bibles and Christian texts, VHS and DVDs," Luiz said. "They were amazed." Each left carrying one copy of every different book and tape under the loose shalwar kammez. They returned two months later with suggestions about which ones were worth the risk of keeping—including what's known as *The Jesus Film*—and what could be discarded. (*The Jesus Film* was produced by Hollywood producer John Heyman with a budget of $6 million, financed primarily by Campus Crusade for Christ. It was released by Warner Brothers in 330 theaters across the United States. While it failed to attract mainstream audiences, it became so popular among evangelicals that it became a mission enterprise, The Jesus Film Project. The movie is said to have reached eight million people, and is celebrated as "one of the greatest evangelistic success stories of all time.")

The material began being distributed by the Afghan converts and church leaders. Then, the Nigerian pastor who had brought his disciples from Ghazni asked for Luiz's help. Rumors of his missionary activities in Afghanistan had led to his dismissal as employee of a multilateral organization. "Nobody wanted to work with him because he had direct contact with the Afghan converts," Luiz said. "But I walked with everyone, because we were all doing God's work." So, Luiz began teaching his disciples too. One Sunday morning, at the weekly meetings of the International Church in Kabul, Luiz met an Afghan and former refugee in the United States, who shared the story of his conversion at a meeting of the Saddleback Church in California, where he had met his wife. The two had decided to move back to Afghanistan to preach the gospel among fellow countrymen, and the church had sponsored them. In Afghanistan, he also served with Franklin Graham's Samaritan's Purse. Many Afghans responded, he later told me, and he needed a safe place to worship and teach the disciples. Luiz immediately agreed to host the group. "Let's do it!"

Most of the converts were Hazaras, an ethnolinguistic minority persecuted by different rulers of Afghanistan on both ethnic and religious grounds. The majority are Shiite Muslim, and the group has lived isolated in the country's central highlands for many centuries. Their features are said to be similar to Mongolian people's, from whom they are believed to be descended, so they tend to stand out, making them an easy target for the ethnic Pashtun Taliban, who are followers of Sunni Islam. Persecution and poverty are said to make Christianity more appealing to Hazaras.

The clandestine house church started with about a dozen members. They met three times a week for Bible study and worship. For safety reasons, the group used codes to schedule the meetings, encrypted messages to communicate with one another, and often changed the time and location of the sessions. As the group grew more confident, the Afghans began bringing friends. Most were students at a university just blocks away. "It started to grow immensely," Luiz said. At its height, the ministry had some seventy Afghan converts, not counting the Nigerian pastor's disciples and the Afghan Christian leaders being trained by Werner. "We knew it was risky. But the Afghans were bringing more people, many of them. And there were no threats yet, but we prayed a lot to God to keep them safe."

The new converts needed to be baptized, so Gis would fill the bathtub at home for the ritual. "I baptized at least fifty-seven of them in the tub, with a bucket, or in the shower," Luiz said. The couple remembers how one Afghan came wearing a mantle specially embroidered for the occasion, with a red cross on the chest like those used by the Knights Templar during the

 Crusades. "I had to explain to him that it was not a good period of Christian history," Luiz said with a laugh.

With more and more new disciples coming in, Luiz considered their home no longer a safe place to perform baptisms. So he started organizing trips to Qargha Lake, an idyllic reservoir about ten miles west of Kabul. Not that the place was much safer, but it would attract less attention than a group of Afghans frequenting the house of a foreigner. The lake would do for the time being. Photos of the ceremonies show Luiz in traditional Afghan clothes and young locals standing in a circle inside the lake with water up to their waists. The new converts were advised how to pretend to be playing a game so that when the Brazilian missionary fully immersed each of them in the water and pulled them out, no one watching would know they were performing a Christian baptism.

One day, Werner and Hannelie were visiting Luiz and Gis for lunch, and the seventy-four-year-old missionary from Europe now renting the lodge in the backyard was to join them. But she never came, so Luiz went to call on her, only to find the woman lying motionless in the bathtub. Hannelie confirmed the woman's death; she likely had died from carbon monoxide emitted from the bukhari heater common in Afghan homes. The old woman had tons of Christian literature in the lodge. The missionaries would have to hide the material somewhere before calling the police. When Gis arrived with the children from school, the police were already at the site. "I thought they had discovered us."

The next day, two men who introduced themselves as officers of the Afghan secret police asked Luiz to come with them and to bring his passport and business license. Luiz gathered Gis and the kids and gave them money, their passports, and a previously written note communicating that he had been imprisoned and the family was on the run. "If I don't return, send this to the church and escape the country with the boys. They will know what to do."

Luckily, Luiz was released a few hours later, but he was now under constant surveillance. A few days later, one of the Christian converts working in the pizzeria received a call from a man who said, *We know what your boss is doing, we know everything about him, and we are going to kill him,* then hung up. Luiz was advised to stay home. That was a difficult task for someone as hyperactive as Luiz, so he bought a bulletproof vest and continued his mission and baptisms. But the stress might have caused his health to decline. Luiz got paratyphoid fever and was bedridden for almost a month. "That was God's providence for me to stay home," he believed. I asked Luiz if he ever thought of giving up and going home. "When the death threats started, yes," he said. "The atmosphere was tense, and I was really down."

In March 2010, a Dutch citizen was detained by the national intelligence and security service of Afghanistan when he landed in Kabul allegedly carrying "illegal material." The man had been Luiz's "Bible smuggler" for years. "He would not stay because it was as dangerous for Europeans as for North Americans, so he would bring the material and leave. He had my phone number registered in his mobile, so the tension was high again," Luiz said. "And this time, it affected the entire [undercover] Christian church in Afghanistan because he had contacts with everyone." Just two months later, a small Afghan-owned private television network named Noorin TV aired two parts of a special report showing Westerners secretly baptizing Afghan converts from Islam to Christianity. Relying on photographs and videos recorded two years before, the news reports showed footage of foreigners and locals worshipping together in Dari. The baptisms and church services, Noorin TV claimed, were presided over "by at least four" foreigners in "secret meetings" held in at least seven "missionary safe houses in western Kabul."

"It denounced everything . . . baptisms, everything!" Luiz said. The scenes had allegedly been discreetly recorded by an Afghan man pretending to be a convert to Christianity. The man filmed using a cell phone and later handed the videos to Noorin TV. The station denounced a "plot to convert Afghanistan to Christianity," with the TV host referring to converts as "infidels." (The same TV channel had in the past said Hitler had discovered a "Jewish plot to dominate the world" and acted to resist Zionism.)

In the footage, a young Afghan man's face can be seen clearly. Others in the group also appeared. "We were involved up to our necks," Luiz said. As soon as the story was aired, Luiz called the young man, who was already on his way to the airport. The following hours were fraught as the Afghan convert tried to leave the country. His face was on every TV set at the airport. He dressed in traditional clothing and used a wool shawl to cover his face, at least partially, hoping to avoid calling anyone's attention.

He bought a ticket to the next flight anywhere in the world (it happened to be Turkey) and left Afghanistan that night. Meanwhile, his American wife quickly packed whatever she could carry, ensuring no Bibles or Christian materials were left behind in case the authorities came to search the house where the couple lived in a village on the outskirts of Kabul. That night, she stayed with Luiz and Gis. They discussed measures to guarantee the safety of the couple's disciples. They also decided she should leave on the first flight available the following day, and they helped her buy the tickets. Luiz would take care of the endangered Christian Afghans. They prayed and cried together.

There was another emergency. "Our house was full of [Christian] material," Luiz said. With Gis and the two boys, Luiz stuffed pillowcases with the recording tape from the Christian VHS cassettes, and destroyed their plastic shells. But they still had to think of what to do with the printed material. Luiz's older son came up with what seemed to be a good solution: to set everything on fire. The family moved all the material hiding in the "Cat's House" into the backyard and dumped it all in the wood-fired clay pizza oven. It turned out to be a bad idea. As the family set it all on fire, clouds of smoke rose from the oven to the sky, resembling those produced by the ever-more-frequent suicide bombings. "We didn't expect it to be so big," Luiz said. Then, according to the family, another miracle happened: A sandstorm suddenly began, which suffocated the fire and covered the ashes. "*É desse jeito!*"

In the following days, Luiz, Werner, and others began a race against time to get the Afghan converts out of the country. The footage of foreigners baptizing Afghans became national news. The Afghan Parliament assembled for an urgent meeting, and lawmakers called for the converts to be convicted under Sharia law. That meant they could be sentenced to death. One legislator said those who appeared in the footage should be "executed in public." Several Afghan authorities and public figures agreed.

 Muslim clerics warned against "the spread of Christianity" and called on President Hamid Karzai to "limit the number of aid workers and Christian missionaries coming to Afghanistan." Massive anti-Christian demonstrations broke out in the main cities across the country. "Long live Islam!" the protesters shouted. In response, President Karzai ordered investigations into proselytizing activities by NGOs.

Surveillance intensified over the next two months, with the offices of Christian organizations turned upside down. Thirteen organizations were labeled as "suspicious," and two—Church World Service and Norwegian Church Aid—were suspended (probably for having the word *church* in their names, as they had no relation with the meetings or the baptisms aired on Noorin TV). Karzai later temporarily banned other NGOs, including Samaritan's Purse. Two international aid workers were deported, but many foreign missionaries and Christian workers had left by then. Afghan converts didn't have that option.

Three months after the TV scandal, ten medical workers, including six Americans, a German, a Briton, and two Afghans working for the International Assistance Mission (IAM), were captured and executed by gunmen in the northeastern province of Badakhshan, where the group was providing eye care in remote villages. It was the worst such attack in the country's history. The Taliban claimed responsibility, saying the medical workers were trying to convert Muslims and were carrying Bibles written in Dari. During the first Taliban regime, Badakhshan had been the only province of Afghanistan not to fall into the hands of the extremists. The attack against the IAM team suggested that there was no longer any safe place for foreigners or Afghans working with them in Afghanistan. IAM's executive director, Dirk Frans, denied proselytizing. The organization had been working in the country for forty-five years, including during the Taliban regime, and the killings underscored the level of danger that Christian organizations now faced in Afghanistan and elsewhere.

According to the Aid Worker Security Database, the number of attacks on humanitarian aid workers worldwide rose sharply in the decade following 2001. Since at least 2006, most violence has occurred in Afghanistan, Sudan, Somalia, and Pakistan, all predominately Muslim countries. Although there is no clear indication that faith-based organizations have been disproportionately singled out, organizations with a clear Christian identity felt more vulnerable.

Luiz and Gis had luckily avoided the worst, but they were lying low, and most evangelical work had been halted for now. Easter was approaching, and Gis invited me to spend Good Friday with the family. There was no sign of the Christian holiday anywhere in Afghanistan, but Fridays are the communal prayer day for Muslims and part of the Afghan weekend, so Luiz and Gis could enjoy the day off. I had scheduled a trip with the International Committee of the Red Cross's physiotherapist, Alberto Cairo, to Badakhshan, where the IAM medical workers had been gunned down. So I thanked Gis for the invitation and promised to call her when I returned to Kabul.

Then, on the morning after I landed back in the capital, my phone rang. "Osama bin Laden is dead," I heard a colleague saying. The news of the US raid in the Pakistani military town of Abbottabad, where bin Laden had been hiding for at least five years, spread like wildfire from Badakhshan's northern hills to Tora Bora's caves. Security alerts popped out on my mobile screen before lines were cut off and the airport was closed.

I went out on the streets and found Kabul as chaotic as usual. Foreign news reported that Afghans were angered by bin Laden's death, but that was not what I saw on the ground. Most ordinary Afghans that I knew personally or had interviewed had no sympathy toward bin Laden, whom they saw as just another foreign player staging proxy wars in ravaged Afghan lands for their own interests, just like the British, the Soviets, the Pakistanis, the Indians, the Iranians, and the Americans.

That same day, I rushed to the Pakistani embassy in Kabul in hopes of getting permission to enter the country, even though the government had imposed a temporary hold on media visas. Three days later, I got the stamp to cross the border into Pakistan.

Holy Warriors

On a Sunday morning in October 2001, just three weeks into the US-led invasion of Afghanistan, six armed men entered the St. Dominic's Roman Catholic Church in the town of Bahawalpur in southern Pakistan and fired automatic rifles into a group of thirty-five Pakistani Protestants, who had no place of worship and had borrowed the building. Sixteen of them died, children included. Sectarian killings involving Sunni and Shiite Muslims were frequent in Pakistan at the time, but never before had a Christian church been the target of such a massive attack. "This is just a start," witnesses heard the men shout before firing.

Anti-American protests broke out in different parts of the country. Spray-painted threats left at the door of Pakistani Christians read "crusaders." In August 2002, four were shot dead in a gun attack on a Christian missionary school north-east of Islamabad. Four days later, a grenade blast killed four and wounded twenty-five at the Christian Hospital Taxila, founded and run by the US-based United Presbyterian Mission. The following month, militants killed seven at a Christian charity in Karachi.

When I landed in Pakistan, Christians were still mourning the assassination of Shahbaz Bhatti, Pakistan's only Christian cabinet minister. Bhatti had been gunned down in Islamabad, his car sprayed with bullets. Before leaving, the assassins threw leaflets signed by the Pakistani Taliban offshoot, which read "Christian infidel."

Bhatti had openly called for reforming Pakistan's draconian blasphemy laws, introduced in the 1980s by the military dictator General Muhammad Zia-ul-Haq, which made perceived offenses against the Prophet Muhammad punishable by death. Two months earlier, Punjab governor Salman Taseer had been shot dead by his security guard for the same reason. Crowds of ordinary Pakistanis rallied in honor of Taseer's killer. Clerics wouldn't say prayers for the governor, even though he was a Muslim.

The murdered politicians had brought the blasphemy law to the center of the debate in Pakistan when Asia Bibi, an impoverished Christian mother, was sentenced to death in November 2010 for allegedly offending the Prophet Muhammad. Bibi had been accused of the crime after offering water to fellow farmhands and having an altercation with a Muslim woman and neighbor who said she wouldn't accept anything from a non-Muslim. Since the law was passed, dozens of Christians have been convicted of "blasphemy."

When I arrived in Pakistan, all Christian schools and churches had closed down since bin Laden's killing for fear of a backlash from militant groups. Days later, on May 6, Al-Qaeda publicly recognized Bin Laden's death. The group congratulated the "Islamic nation" for "the martyrdom of its good son Osama" and promised Americans that "their joy will turn to sorrow and their tears will mix with blood." The focus of the global jihad was still on the "far enemy," but Christians in Pakistan had become a closer, easier target for revenge.

In October 2012, I returned to Pakistan to cover the attempted assassination of Malala Yousafzai, a fourteen-year-old activist for girls' education and a devoted Muslim. On the way back from the Swat Valley, where Malala lived, I stopped in Peshawar to see the Reverend Zia Pervez Mirza, the historic All Saints Church minister. We met at the restaurant of the Pearl Continental Hotel. In 2009, gunmen riding in a pickup truck laden with explosives had attacked the landmark hotel, killing at least seventeen people and injuring dozens with glass shrapnel. The explosion was so intense it left a fifteen-foot crater on the ground and caused the building to partially collapse. The hotel was popular among diplomats, aid workers, Western journalists, and spies. A Serbian working for UNCHR and a Filipino with UNICEF were dead. The UN pulled its staff from Peshawar immediately after the attack, and to this day, several aid agencies consider the city off-limits.

The hotel was still under reconstruction, so I met Zia at the recently reopened restaurant. He was visibly tense, frequently looking around us. His voice was almost inaudible amid the clatter of dishes and silverware. Born to a nominal Christian family, Zia grew up running up and down the corridors of the Mission Hospital in Peshawar, where his mother was a nurse. (The hospital had been founded by missionaries to treat leprosy patients during the British Raj.) In his youth, he became attracted to Marxist ideals and joined the Communist Party of Pakistan. When Zia and his wife, Teresa, lost two newborn sons to undiagnosed causes, the grieving couple found comfort in the church. "I was 'born again' in 1985, after I lost our first two baby boys, one after the other," Zia said. "Something . . . definitely the Holy Spirit led me to read the Bible. That, in turn, brought me to life in Jesus. Then God gave us a new life."

That happened during the anti-Soviet Afghan War, when millions of refugees poured into camps at the border with Pakistan. Zia and Teresa started a "home church," which, in fact, met at the Mission Hospital. The hospital ran emergency health centers for Afghan refugees, mobile clinics in the war zones, and treated the most seriously injured mujahedeen. And Zia welcomed them to his church fellowship. "It wasn't easy," Zia said. "They would come and just sit there." Zia began assisting US Christian organizations and relief agencies in reaching the refugees at the border between Afghanistan and Pakistan. "Many of them would just come for food, and we definitely wanted to feed them," he said. But Zia noticed that some refugees sent to him for Bible study did not really want to convert. They often lied about their Muslim identities, hoping that being a Christian would give them better access to aid. "I'd tell them, please don't hide your identity. You are a Muslim, and you are welcome. You don't need to say you are a Christian to receive aid. Now, this is a Bible study. If you wish, you can come." Some, in fact, did.

One of them was Hussain, who later met Luiz in Afghanistan. During the Afghan civil war and subsequent Taliban regime, Hussain had lived with his family in the Khurasan camp, which sheltered thousands of Afghans for almost two decades, and had become a breeding ground for both mujahedeen recruiters and soul-searching Christians.

I later met Hussain in Kabul, and he told me how he became a Christian. "I was living in a tent with my wife and children. They were hungry and desperate," he said. A few meters from his tent was a stream of scarce water, contaminated with sewage. One night, Hussain dreamed that something was blocking the flow of the stream. "Then, I saw a book with a red cover, and as this book floated with the stream, it cleaned the water, turning it crystal clear," he said, bursting into tears in front of me. "I found it so beautiful."

A few days later, Hussain recalled, an aid worker came to his tent, handed him packs of emergency food rations for the family, and left. In between the boxes, Hussain found a copy of the Bible, with a red cover. "It was the book I had seen in my dream, so I started reading it that same night and didn't stop until I finished," he told me. When the aid worker returned to supply the family with a new food pack, Hussain shared the story with him. Soon after, Zia came to visit him. "They told me that there was this man interested in hearing about Jesus, but aid workers couldn't openly proselytize, so they sent me to him. Hussain would ask me to come again and again. Then, he started coming to our house church and became very committed," Zia told me. "He never asked me for anything, like money or . . . anything!"

At Zia's "house church," Hussain met other Pakistani converts to Christianity. Bassat and Sajad had both been raised as devout Muslims; Bassat was a maulana, a respected religious scholar and Muslim leader; Sajad had, in his youth, allegedly joined the feared sectarian group Sipah-e-Sahaba Pakistan, responsible for a series of murderous attacks against Shia

 Muslims and Christians. The two men were originally from Quetta, the capital of Baluchistan province, which had become a terrorist haven.

Historically, Baluchistan was a secular province, but only a tiny, reclusive, and fearful Christian community survived in Quetta. They had been the target of attacks and death threats. Some had recently received letters from militant Sunni groups to either convert to Islam, leave, or die, Zia told me. As an ethnic Balochi, Bassat blended in well among church members. So, he started attending the All Saints Church, where Zia was a pastor. Hussain and Sajad were Pashtun, the dominant ethnic group living across the Afghanistan-Pakistan border that included the Taliban leadership. So, Zia started giving them private Bible classes at his own home in Peshawar.

When the new influx of Christian aid organizations arrived in the aftermath of September 11 and the US invasion of Afghanistan, Zia again became their host in the tribal areas of Pakistan. That's how he met a Brazilian evangelical and, like Luiz and Gis, a disciple of Pastor Vinci Barros's. She had joined Barros's house church in their hometown of Vitoria, and she later moved to Europe, joining World in Need, which sent her as a missionary to Afghanistan. At the time, she was managing the construction of Cure Hospital, in Kabul, part of a Christian faith-based network of pediatric surgical hospitals operating in a dozen countries. She often crossed the border into Pakistan to buy material and solve administrative issues, as infrastructure and banking were precarious in the early years of the war in Afghanistan.

In Peshawar, fellow Christians suggested she come to Zia. Zia assigned Hussain and Sajad to help her navigate the siege city of Peshawar and to accompany her anywhere she needed to go, as it was dangerous and considered culturally inappropriate for a woman to walk alone in the tribal areas of Pakistan. The Pakistani pastor later became WIN's representative in the country and frequently traveled to Kabul to minister to converted returnees, like Hussain, and give other Afghans "the opportunity to hear the Good News." Many of his disciples had moved back to Afghanistan, but there were no churches in their war-ravaged homeland. So Reverend Zia ministered to them.

The US alliance with Pakistan and the growing number of strikes by the American military against targets in the tribal areas neighboring Afghanistan fueled violent Islamic militancy on both sides of the border. That was especially the case after the US began relying on drones to conduct bombings, which intensified after 2008 under President Obama.

Between 2001 and 2007, there were 15 suicide bombings in Pakistan, but in the subsequent six years, the number jumped to 358—the highest anywhere in the world. By 2012, there had been more than 1,400 terrorist attacks since the beginning of the year, more than in Iraq and Afghanistan. The violent militant upsurge turned Pakistan's tribal areas into a no-man's-land. "It has never been as dangerous as it is now," Zia told me. "In the last five, six years, since the emergence of the Taliban here, things have changed."

Most churches in this area date from the British Raj and have survived untouched for centuries. Christians used to decorate their homes and church buildings for Christmas, but many now worry about the risks. "I worked with Muslims in a bank for twenty-six years, and I would joke with them about faith, and they wouldn't mind," Zia said. "In the past, attacks were sporadic." I asked him if there had been threats against him or his disciples. "Oh, so many! So, so many! Churches exploded, and pastors were murdered," Zia responded. "Two of my most loyal disciples, whom I deeply cared for, were kidnapped and killed."

According to Zia, Bassat had been receiving death threats for having converted to Christianity. One day, he simply disappeared. Abductions had become endemic in Pakistan, with several cases reported, mostly of Christian girls and women kidnapped and forced to marry a Muslim man and convert to Islam.

Sajad, Zia's closest disciple, who had married the pastor's sister-in-law, was kidnapped and tortured twice. Days after his third abduction, Sajad's body was left in Zia's front yard. "We saw something horrible," Zia said, recounting how he and his wife found Sajad's deformed body. The evangelical couple took their friend's heavy, dead body inside and gave him the final bath. "His testicles were crushed. Too much torture . . ." Zia said. That same night, he rented a wagon, took the body to a Christian hospital that issued the death certificate, and buried his friend and brother-in-law in a Christian cemetery in Faisalabad.

Zia believed that the kidnappers were Islamic militants of Sipah-e-Sahaba, which Sajad had been a member of before converting to Christianity. Like Sajad, the reverend had received threats from the group for ministering to Christians who had Muslim backgrounds. But Zia would never know the truth. "We couldn't call the police or ask for an investigation. Even reporting his murder would be dangerous because the police would want to know why he was killed and left in our yard." And, in doing so, they'd uncover Zia's missionary work among Muslims.

"He [Sajad] was a sharp man, and I always told him: Jesus doesn't want you to be a martyr. Please, live! Be peaceful. Look for opportunities. But he . . . he would go to the maulanas and argue with them [in defense of Christianity as the true religion vs. Islam]," Zia said, lowering his head. "They were very committed [Christians], and I miss them very much." Zia took a deep breath and continued: "It is not easy to be a [Christian] Pakistani. . . . And evangelicals won't hide their faith. But the time comes when you have to . . . this is true even for traditional Christians in Pakistan. And it is all more dangerous for those converted from Islam. Most of them are secret believers and still have to go to the mosque."

Hussain, Zia's disciple assigned to help the Brazilian aid worker serving with World in Need, had escaped what he believed to have been an attempted kidnapping and survived an attack from unknown assailants who shot at him from inside a car. Soon after Sajad's death, Hussain moved back to Afghanistan and began assisting WIN's aid work. Zia often visited Hussain in Kabul, but escalating violence prevented him from crossing the border in the four years after 2008, leading WIN to close its doors in Afghanistan. Hussain remained in Kabul and started serving with Shelter Now, where he met Luiz, Gis, Werner, and Hannelie. He later brought his wife and children back home to Kabul. Some of them became disciples of S. P. Luiz, and employees at his pizza-delivery business.

Zia continued serving as a pastor at the All Saints Church in Peshawar. The historic church was modeled on Indian Saracenic architecture that derived from the great Muslim civilizations. Its front door was oriented toward Mecca. One can see the minaret and dome rise above Peshawar from a distance. I asked Zia if he, too, feared going to church these days. "Oh, no, no. This church has been here since 1883. We have one thousand and five hundred members. Of course, we have guards there, and the security has been improved recently."

The garrisoned church was surrounded by a barbed wire fence, cement blocks, and rings of sandbags. Before reaching the church, visitors had to pass through a security checkpoint, and there were armed guards at the gate. Nonetheless, on September 22, 2013, two men shot the guards at the entrance and rushed toward the crowd of believers leaving the church after Zia's Sunday service. They detonated explosive vests amid the worshippers, killing at least 127 people and wounding more than 250. Rickshaws and man-driven carts helped carry the victims' bodies to the hospitals and the morgue while ambulances tried to beat the traffic entering the Kohati gate. Among the injured were thirty-seven children. Jundul Hafsa, a Pakistani Taliban associate, claimed responsibility and stated that the attack was in retaliation against US drone strikes.

Zia survived the attack, but chemical agents used in the explosives left him with severe skin lesions that caused lasting pain. He died in 2019 while in the hospital for one of many skin treatments he had to undergo. The All Saints Church suicide bombing was the deadliest attack on Christians in the history of Pakistan.

From a Mission Field to a Mission Force

In late 2012, I traveled to Indonesia to meet Luis Bush, who was arguably the person most responsible for inspiring thousands of people like Luiz and Werner to leave their home countries to evangelize in the 10/40 Window. Bush was hosting an underground summit of Christian evangelical leaders from around the world to discuss current threats to the spread of Christianity, notably the rise of terrorism, and to design a plan for global missions in the subsequent seven years. The morning I landed, a forty-year-old man entered the Simanosor Maranatha Batak Protestant Church in North Sumatra wielding a machete and struck the children attending the service, killing three and severely injuring several others. A mob of villagers raided homes in the hunt for the attacker and stoned him to death.

The meeting was held in Denpasar, the capital of Bali, known for its beaches, popular resorts, and lively entertainment scene. Since 2002, it was also known as the site of the triple bombings that killed 202 people in the first major terrorist attack against foreign targets since 9/11. The Al-Qaeda affiliate

 Jemaah Islamiyah, considered Asia's most dangerous terrorist network, claimed responsibility for the attacks. After the Bali bombings, Indonesia's Detachment 88 counterterrorism unit had succeeded in dismantling the organization, but not their ideology.

The terrorists were obviously only a few among millions of Muslims. But, they were part of a much larger tide of rising religious conservativism in Indonesia and elsewhere across the Islamic world. "A deep pain seems to be going already for a long time in the hearts of several Christian leaders seeing the 'powerlessness' of the Christian communities," read the message in the conference booklet, pointing to increasing hostilities and persecution against Christians in the Middle East and in countries like Pakistan, China, and India as well as in Indonesia.

Access to the Transform World Global Challenges Summit was by invitation only. Applications were "prayerfully screened." Most of the delegates were under fifty, and had previously been asked to demonstrate their desire and ability to commit to a seven-year plan to seek "His Kingdom purposes." Amid Balinese dancers, traditional food, and heartfelt prayers at the "spiritual" welcome ceremony, Luis Bush saluted from the stage an audience of some five hundred key leaders of the global mission movement from at least fifty countries.

"We are here to decide what should be done in the next seven years," Bush told the audience. "We confess that we cannot change even one soul with our own effort alone." In fact, Bush's efforts alone had redirected thousands upon thousands of missionaries, mainly from Latin America, into perilous terrains inside the rectangular area of North Africa, the Middle

East, and Asia, the "resistant belt" preventing Christians from finishing the Great Commission.

The 10/40 Window had become the central catalytic movement for global evangelism. In evangelical circles, Bush was seen as a "missional hero," at times compared with American evangelist and Nobel Peace Prize laureate John R. Mott, chairman of the historic Student Volunteer Movement. The late American theologian C. Peter Wagner regarded Bush as "the most influential" evangelist in the cause of global missions.

Most importantly, his prophecy that Latin America would become a mission force was now a reality. In the following years, the number of Latino and non-Western missionaries continued growing, while the number of Western missionaries declined. "In the aftermath of the Lausanne Movement, American missionaries started to transfer the leadership of the local churches to the hands of Brazilian pastors for the first time," the representative of Bush's Transform the World initiative and Window 10/40 in Latin America told me. "But the Americans never believed that Brazilians could be missionaries. That was all on Dr. Bush."

The first delegate that Bush introduced to me was a prominent young leader of the mission movement named Maisel Rocha. A Baptist born to a poor family in the northeast of Brazil, Rocha dreamed of pursuing a military career until he read a pamphlet at his evangelical church calling young believers to evangelize Muslims in North Africa and decided instead to "fight" for souls. Rocha integrated the first team of the Radical Program started in 2001 by Missão Horizontes, one of the first Brazilian missions agencies to send native missionaries overseas. After attending training sections in Paraguay and Brazil, and spending a period in the UK and France learning English and French, Rocha was sent to Niger, where he served for three years.

The Radical Program's first group had a weeklong ministry with Luis and Doris Bush as part of their training, before leaving for Northern Africa. The majority of participants later return to the field as career missionaries, particularly among Muslim peoples. One of the instructors for Missão Horizontes was American evangelist Joshua Lingel, the founder and president of i2 Ministries, which he started in 2003 to equip Christians to "establish a global mission force to effectively evangelize Muslims." i2 Ministries claimed to have trained "a network of over 20,000 churches in Asia, Africa, and South America" in "Muslim Ministry and Islamic Studies."

At the summit in Bali, Lingel led the flocks registered for the "Ideological Challenge," and I joined them. Behind closed doors, the days started with a prayer: "We ask God for the liberation of those souls from Islam. Release them from the darkness and deception," one delegate said. "We want to see the Muslims glorifying Your name," another added.

The group's focus in Bush's Transform the World's seven-year plan was on countering the advance of Islam. "Why should we care about the Muslims?" Lingel asked the group. "Well, the answer is very simple: because God, God loves us.... He wants them delivered from false religion."

Under Lingel's guidance, in 2007 Rocha started the Missão Mundo Muçulmano—M3 (Muslim World Mission), the Brazilian branch of the American i2 Ministries. In the four years leading up to 2011, M3 had trained some nine hundred Brazilians who were serving or about to be sent to Muslim fields. (The next year, when I met Rocha again at another conference, he claimed the number had jumped to four thousand.) In Bali, Rocha was excited about a new project he was overseeing for i2Ministries: the production of a 350-hour-long video course about Islam.

Originally filmed in English, the video course would be translated by Rocha's team at M3 and sent to native evangelical missionaries in seven Portuguese-speaking countries. Rocha showed me a few scenes filmed in the coastal dunes of Natal, in Brazil's far northeast, which to him resembled the Middle East's deserts. He was also planning to recruit and train armchair missionaries, especially retired evangelicals who, as described by Rocha, had "all the time in the world." Their job was to respond to anti-Christian Islamic rhetoric on television, radio, and social media networks. They "preached the gospel from the comfort of their homes," Joshua Lingel said to the group in Bali. "You can do it twenty-four hours a day."

"Luis calls people together," Peruvian evangelist Ricardo Luna told me during an interview one afternoon during the summit. Luna was then the director of the Confederación Evangélica Latinoamericana (Conela), representing over 487,000 churches around the world. The advantages of sending a Latino rather than an American to preach among Muslims, in Luna's view, were clear. "We don't require as many funds, and we are more culturally relevant to the Middle East. We don't want to change their culture. We celebrate it," he said. Perhaps more important, when Latin American missionaries go on missions, "the cross doesn't come with the sword."

Among Latin Americans, Brazilians stand out as coming from the largest and richest country in the region, and a trade partner of the Muslim world—Brazil is the world's top supplier of halal meat. Its traditional neutral position in world affairs, conciliatory diplomacy, and absence from wars contributed to Brazilians being especially welcomed by Muslims. "[Americans] are better in planting churches, discipleship, and establishing local leaders," said Rocha. "But [Brazilians] win hearts and minds."

Then, there is soccer. "He can wear a T-shirt that reads 'Jesus Loves You.' But, if I do, I'd serve a long term in prison," said the leader of the Lausanne Movement in Asia, who asked not to be named for safety reasons. He held up a picture of a Brazilian missionary and soccer coach serving in Malaysia. "Football . . . opens the doors," he said, asserting that Brazilians were successfully preaching in Thailand, China, Laos, and Myanmar with the help of soccer. "They love Brazil, and they love football."

The Blood of the Martyrs Are the Seeds of the Church

"Know Jesus?" asked the driver of the rusty taxi rattling its way through Kabul. One year had passed since the killing of Osama bin Laden, and there were visibly more police officers than before on the streets of the Afghan capital. The extra checkpoints slowed the traffic flow. Giant cement blocks advanced halfway into the pathway, keeping suicide bombers away from foreign embassies and government buildings.

"Know Jesus?" the Afghan driver repeated, turning to me in the back. Jesus? That Jesus? "Yes, Jesus. Nice man!" he responded. He had earphones and listened to the Audio Holy Bible in Dari playing on his mobile phone on an SD card smuggled into the country by missionaries. Preaching in Afghanistan had become even more dangerous, but technology helped. Salvation now came in the form of a chip.

I had returned to Afghanistan to learn about the fate of the Afghan Christian converts persecuted after the Noorin TV affair. According to the US Department of State's annual Report to Congress on International Religious Freedom, twenty-six

Christian Afghans were jailed after the news broke, after being arrested in government and police raids on Christian NGOs' offices and guesthouses. Luiz had spent the subsequent months visiting prisons, trying to secure their release, and smuggling other Christian converts out of the country.

Spring recess was near, so my first stop that morning was at the school run by the Brazilian missionaries. The taxi driver was the fiancé of the school's director, and he had been sent to fetch me. The couple had been engaged for eight months, but she had not yet fully disclosed to him that she was a Christian convert from Islam. Instead, she had gradually and discreetly introduced him to the matter by suggesting that he listen to audiobooks with "beautiful stories," like the Bible.

Unlike other foreign enterprises, the school had no armed security. Cocó Nasir, as the Brazilians kindly called the chowkidar, had been informed about my visit and allowed me in. Children wearing traditional Afghan sandals and slippers played soccer on a shabby open sports court in the front yard.

Gis greeted me in the yard with her usual smile and warm welcome, and guided me on a tour around the school. In one classroom with salmon-painted walls and colorful hanging drawings, fourteen children struggled to stay seated on the tiny wooden chairs in the presence of a stranger. In another schoolroom, a young Afghan named Najeeb taught boys and girls how to write their names in the Western alphabet—Mostafa, Shamila, Maryam, Ashraf, Yaser, and Tina.

There was a traditional Afghan communal seating room with cushions, rugs, and low tables; a teachers' room featuring just a sink, where Brazilian coffee and table water were served; and one bathroom with an Indian-style squat toilet shared by the foreign missionaries, the Afghan staff, and the kids. The furniture was simple and unmatched—all items were second-hand and had been donated by Western missionaries, friends, and family. Perhaps most notable in the school dêcor was the absence of Christian symbols.

Cross-shaped structures, crucifixes, or Bibles were nowhere to be seen. As in any Afghan public school, the girls wore white hijab, and classes were gender-segregated for children from sixth grade and up. The school had 130 Afghan kids enrolled in pre-kindergarten and after-school programs. Classes included English, Portuguese, computing, arts, capoeira, and soccer, all taught by a mix of volunteering foreign missionaries and salaried Afghan teachers.

Gis introduced me to Fatema, a young Brazilian missionary who had arrived a few months before with her husband, Henrique. They were being trained to replace Luiz and Gis, who were moving on to Iraq. Raised by nominally Catholic parents, Fatema had converted to evangelical Christianity. She became a missionary after a Campus Crusade team preached the gospel at her university. (Campus Crusade was founded in 1951 by American missionaries Bill and Vonette Bright at the University of California. As of 2023, it had grown to more than five thousand ministries in universities worldwide.)

Henrique grew up attending a Brazilian native missionary church inspired by the International House of Prayer in Kansas City. The two met at a mission school in the state of Goias. Henrique became a missionary to the *ribeirinhos* (traditional communities formed by riverside peoples in Brazil), while Fatema's church sent her to Nepal, where she met Luiz at a missions conference. Upon her return to Brazil, Fatema and

Henrique married. One day, Luiz called them and said he needed more hands in Afghanistan. Soon after, Henrique's church agreed to sponsor the couple as missionaries, and they became Luiz and Gis's disciples in Kabul. Fatema took Dari classes at the school and taught English in return.

Fatema was tall with a curvy body and a strong presence. She had straight, long, dark hair; brown eyes, which looked smaller behind large round glasses; and a comprehensive and captivating smile. That morning, she felt elated and particularly excited. Tamana, a twenty-two-year-old Muslim and her Dari teacher, had just told her about a "bearded man dressed in white cloths and involved in bright light" who had appeared to her while she was sleeping. The recently arrived Brazilian missionary was convinced that it had not been a dream, but a vision with Jesus. If it went well, Tamana would become her second Afghan disciple. The first was Faranoz, daughter of Nasir, the chowkidar.

Fatema and Henrique liked to walk to the school. Both spoke Arabic, wore traditional Afghan clothing, and had physical features similar to Arabs. Henrique had grown a long steel wool—like beard.

Gis's School of the Future continued to be operated under Partnership in Academics and Development (PAD), directed by Werner Groenewald, the South African pastor and missionary living with his wife and two children in Kabul. But no funds came from the organization. Luiz's and Werner's families had their basic living expenses covered by churches in Brazil and South Africa. Everything else depended on their ability to fundraise or run profitable businesses. Believers from the church in Brazil and elsewhere could "adopt" a student at the School of the Future for $25 a month, but the donations from the church in Brazil had always been insufficient.

Luiz had just returned from India after visiting twelve Afghan converts whom the missionaries had managed to smuggle out of Afghanistan before the police could arrest them following the Noorin TV scandal. The group had settled in a suburb south of Delhi, and the Brazilian missionary was thrilled with what he had seen there: The Afghan converts had started a congregation of their own in the refuge, and the Afghan church was booming. "They are still doing God's work in India, Pakistan, and the Philippines," he told me excitedly.

One night, we were invited to dinner at the Soviet-era apartment of an American pastor named Bill Lynch, who had traveled with Luiz to India. At the time, he was planning to start a Bible school run by Luke, a local convert who used his Christian name. Luke had been among those jailed after the Noorin TV affair.

At the time of his detention, Luke was in a guesthouse shared with a young Brazilian missionary in Herat, where they served with Shelter Now. They were surprised when the police arrived during a night raid. The policemen took Luke, while she was left behind. He was taken to Pul-e-Charki, Afghanistan's largest and most feared detention center. "They'd hit me in all parts of the body and constantly threaten to behead me," he told me. "I'd say to them: 'You can kill me; it doesn't matter, for I am saved.'" Upon his release, more than six months later, he escaped to India and stayed there until things calmed down in Afghanistan. Now he was back to Afghanistan, but living in another province under a false identity. His time in prison had deeply impacted him and the entire family. "I am too scared to share the gospel now." Nevertheless, he was willing to head Lynch's Bible School for Afghan converts.

This was my third trip to Afghanistan, and the change in mood in the country was clear. The Taliban was stronger than ever, while the US-backed government of President Hamid Karzai was drowning in corruption scandals. Even more challenging was the fact that the Taliban had recovered large parts of the country's territory. They seemed to be winning the hearts and minds of the Afghan people in the Pashtun south and the Pashtun enclaves in the north. The US had lost credibility for failing to stabilize and rebuild Afghanistan. It was blamed for the chaos and the widespread violence, especially in the tribal areas of the border with Pakistan, where drone attacks had killed innocent civilians. Rural villages had turned into fertile grounds for recruitment from the different factions that had fought the civil war and had begun preparing their forces for when the American troops left. In the cities, the mood among ordinary Afghans had shifted from hope and relief to anger and despair.

On Friday, as Afghans prepared for the weekly prayer day at their mosques, we left for Werner and Hannelie's home, where the South African pastor hosted a Christian service for a small group of devoted missionaries who remained in Kabul. The living room had been arranged for the religious service with a few chairs, but most of the dozen adults already present sat on the floor. A young man played the guitar next to his veiled wife, singing gospel rhymes while trying to handle the couple's four small children. A wood-fired bukhari kept the living room warm. Smoke from the chimney painted the wall with a fine layer of ash. Strips of plastic covered the window cracks, both to keep the cold air outside and the Jesus songs and worship inside.

Werner began the service with a heartfelt welcome. He thanked everyone for coming despite the risks. He read stretches of the Bible in English, while some tried to follow with versions of the book in Dari and Pashto. Vigorous praying and singing followed. Then, all the children were guided upstairs, where they were kept busy playing Bible crossword puzzles and Christmas bingo with Jean-Pierre and Rhodé. After the prayers, the adults discussed the missionary efforts in Afghanistan, which had come to a stop following the Noorin TV scandal.

Werner revealed that he had secretly met with a few Afghan church leaders. The South African pastor hoped to empower them to resume Bible teachings and church meetings. "The Afghan church leaders are scared. It has become too risky for them to gather with foreigners. They believe the secret police is still watching them," Luiz said. "So, we [foreigners] must overcome our fears and do more for them." "The church is as big here as we make it," Werner agreed. "We have to break our fears and go out and talk to people and heal the people," Luiz continued. "God has a purpose for Afghanistan. But He operates through us. If we are too scared, His plans cannot be fulfilled."

"Churches [outside Afghanistan] are full of believers, but they also worship other gods, like consumerism," Werner said. "Here, we've lost followers, but that is good because only those firm in their faith remain." Not long after, in late 2012, Luiz and Gis left Afghanistan. Hussain and other converts—including those who had been jailed after the Noorin TV scandal, the Afghans working in the pizzeria and at the missionary's school, as well as Werner and other internationals—all came to say goodbye. They didn't know at the time, but the farewell party would be the last gathering of foreign and local missionaries in Afghanistan.

Not long after, Werner and Hannelie received a short visit from one of the Dutch Reformed Church's reverends, who carried a letter informing them that the church had decided to cut their support by nearly half. South Africa was reeling from the global financial crisis, and the church was struggling to stay afloat.

By 2013, Werner and Hannelie could no longer afford the rent for the spacious house, so they moved with Jean-Pierre and Rhodé to PAD's office. The family occupied the rooms upstairs, while the NGO's office was rearranged on the ground floor. Werner's church meetings were transferred to a windowless basement. Hannelie started working as a private doctor at a clinic and a hospital in Kabul, and returned to homeschooling the children. Jean-Pierre was crushed about leaving the international school, becoming isolated from friends and increasingly unhappy. Rhodé's back pains intensified.

After seven years in Afghanistan, Luiz and Gis had moved on to a new mission abroad, so the family had lost their best friends. One morning, Werner told Hannelie that he was considering leaving Afghanistan.

Earlier in 2014, the United States had announced that NATO's combat mission in Afghanistan would officially end on the last day of the year. A newly formed government led by President Ashraf Ghani had just taken office without being able to control most of the country. Militant groups were emboldened and waging attacks against security forces.

On Saturday, November 29, there were rumors that an insurgent group was planning an incursion into the capital. Hannelie didn't usually work on Saturdays, but the hospital called her in because of the heightened alert. As the day went on, the atmosphere remained unexpectedly calm. The apprehension of an attack faded. After attending to a few patients in the afternoon, Hannelie called the hospital's driver to take her home. Shortly after 4:00 p.m., the driver received a phone call: There was an attack at the house.

Hannelie tried to call her husband, but Werner didn't pick up. She tried to call the kids, but Jean-Pierre and Rhodé didn't answer either. The traffic was jammed as usual, but the journey home from the clinic felt like forever this time. As the car approached the PAD office, Hannelie saw that the street was sealed off, so she got out and walked toward the house. Afghan policemen blocked her way. For about an hour, she walked around the block, searching for a place from which she could see her home. She found one, but nothing seemed to be happening there. Terrorist attacks were part of the routine for anyone living in Afghanistan, so she thought: *They must be hiding in their rooms.*

The sun was setting when armored vehicles approached the street. Suddenly, heavy gunshots were fired, followed by a loud explosion. The neighborhood darkened. A police officer guided Hannelie to an office nearby where she could take shelter. Gunshots and explosions continued for another hour, and Hannelie could see her house burning.

Luiz and Gis were about to leave for Egypt on their first field trip as part of the couple's new mission assisting Brazilian missionaries stationed in the Muslim world. I was about to accompany them when they sent me a message from the airport in Scotland: "The Taliban is at Hannelie's house," Gis wrote. "Family hostage." At about 7:30 p.m., a friend called Hannelie from Dubai and told her that the news channel Al Jazeera had just spoken to someone inside the house and been told the six hostages had been safely released. "Thank [the] Lord," Hannelie sighed.

But then, another friend called and asked to come to meet her. As he approached, Hannelie noticed he was crying. "This is going to be the longest night of your life," he told Hannelie. "They are all dead."

Five hours earlier, an armed man dressed in a police uniform had jumped the wall outside the PAD office and opened the front door to let two others in. Hassan, the Afghan gatekeeper, was gunned down before he could react. Inside the house, Werner was expecting visitors for a church meeting. When he heard shots, he gathered his Afghan staff and told everyone to hide. He ran upstairs to his children, who were in their rooms on the first floor. But he encountered the gunmen, who shot Werner twice and left him bleeding to death. The Afghans in the basement heard the children scream, and a flurry of shots followed. The attackers returned downstairs and sprayed bullets inside a tiny room, killing one of the staff members. The people in the basement heard one of the gunmen say: "We've killed them all." The terrorists were on a suicide mission and had been ordered to fight the security forces for as long as they could and not leave the house alive, so they waited for police and soldiers to arrive. The firefight lasted for some three and a half hours until the terrorists were dead.

The Taliban claimed responsibility for the attack, saying the compound belonged to a "secret Christian missionary group." Werner was forty-six, Jean-Pierre was seventeen, and Rhodé was just fifteen.

"I couldn't register what they told me," Hannelie later told me. She didn't say anything or even cry as she heard the news, and followed the missionaries to their home in silence and shock. From there, she called her sister to ask her to inform their parents. Then she called Werner's mother, who hung up after hearing the news. "I wasn't thinking," Hannelie said. "It was like in hypnosis. I was clinging to God." Later that night, Hannelie walked to the bathroom and vomited.

The following day, Hannelie went to the house to see what was left, and found everything burned to ashes. "But the miracle was that the fire stopped at Jean-Pierre's bedroom," she said. Her two kids were killed there, and Hannelie concluded, "God wanted to have their bodies preserved."

Before Hannelie could bring the bodies back to South Africa, she had to help prepare them to be transferred and buried because no one else in the clinic knew "the Christian way." "I had to embalm my family. I had to take care of everything. There were four doctors; one came in the evening. He washed them, checked the entrance and exit wounds, and I helped embalm the bodies," she said. "I told them that I forgave the Taliban."

Fatema and Henrique were in Brazil, where she had just given birth to the couple's first child three weeks before. They were waiting to vaccinate the newborn before returning to Kabul. Their most trusted Afghan converts had been left in charge of the school and the pizza-delivery business. But given the school's links with PAD, the Afghans were too frightened to return to the compound to collect documents, computers, or anything else after the attack. The mullah of a local mosque agreed to accompany an Afghan convert to the school to pack up whatever the two could carry. Nasir collected Henrique's and Fatema's belongings at their Kabul home to be shipped back to Brazil.

The mission in Afghanistan was over.

In December 2014, I met Luiz and Gis as we flew to Pretoria, South Africa, for the funeral of Werner, Jean-Pierre, and Rhodé . The couple greeted me with a smile before Gis burst into tears. Luiz confessed he felt disappointed. "With God?" I asked. "Yes," he said, though not for the reasons I thought. "I am disappointed with God for allowing me to leave. . . . I wanted to be in Afghanistan now because Werner and I were the only ones doing God's work. He was the last one of us."

At the site of Werner, Jean-Pierre, and Rhodé's graves in Pretoria East Cemetery, a sign reads: "They Tried to Bury Us. They Didn't Know We Were Seeds."

The Church Revolution

Muna, a Brazilian evangelical missionary, was home in Cairo with her three children when gunshots sounded. Her husband, Sobhy, had crossed the border into Israel, taking Christian pilgrims to the Holy Land. Egypt had been home to the family since 2007. The leafy neighborhood where they lived, south of Cairo, lies on the east bank of the Nile River, from where Christians believe Mary and Joseph embarked on a sailing boat with baby Jesus, fleeing persecution. A church and monastery mark the site where the Holy Family is believed to have departed. At the church's sanctuary, a Bible displayed behind glass was allegedly found floating on the Nile River open to Isaiah 19:25—"Blessed be Egypt, my people."

When Muna heard the first shots, she threw herself to the kitchen floor, shielding the children. It was the early days of the 2011 revolution, when the Egyptian people took over Tahrir Square in central Cairo, calling for the resignation of autocratic president Hosni Mubarak. The upheaval in Egypt followed a twenty-eight-day campaign of civil resistance and street demonstrations in Tunisia that led to the ousting of longtime president Zine El Abidine Ben Ali, which then spread across Arab countries.

That afternoon, gangs of thugs roamed the neighborhood, spreading chaos, setting vehicles and buildings on fire, breaking into supermarkets, shops, and banks, and threatening residents and foreigners in what antigovernment demonstrators saw as a government-planned attempt to disrupt the protests. Egyptian policemen were nowhere to be seen. Soon, male residents appeared on the streets armed with machetes, sticks, poles, knives, and even a sword, trying to secure property and protect family members and neighbors from looters. Some dragged concrete blocks to the middle of the streets while others hid behind makeshift barricades. The sound of gunfire made the once-quiet suburb sound like a war zone. "We couldn't stand the smell of gunpowder," Muna told me.

The Egyptian government had blocked all communications across the country. After trying unsuccessfully to reach her husband on the phone, Muna told the kids to wait and rushed to the bedroom, hiding all the evangelizing material she had. She packed essential items, passports, and cash. *But where should I go?* Muna thought. "I felt lost," she recalled. "I was contaminated with fear." Muna knelt on the bedroom floor, holding a Bible. It opened at Daniel 2:21: "He removes kings and raises kings," she read, interpreting the passage as a reminder that "God is in control." She returned to the kids and said firmly: "We are not going anywhere. Your father isn't here, but God is with us."

The ruler of Egypt for thirty years, Mubarak had long exploited Western fears of Islamic extremists taking power. While Mubarak created a front against terrorism, he also allowed hard-liners to continue operating as long as they didn't threaten the regime. Worrying that the untrustworthy but necessary ally could be replaced by a hostile government, leaders of Western nations were cautious about supporting the uprising. When communication was reestablished, Muna wrote to the church in Brazil: "Pray for Egypt."

But this revolution was different. Egyptian protesters demanded democratic reforms, social justice, and the rule of law. They were primarily young, craving freedom and socio-economic opportunities in a globalized and increasingly interconnected world. They didn't burn American flags or chant anti-imperialist slogans. Images of Osama bin Laden or his Egyptian successor, Ayman al-Zawahiri, were nowhere to be seen.

The following Friday, a massive and defiant crowd gathered in even larger numbers at Tahrir Square than the previous week. In a demonstration of people's unity, Christians in the crowd formed a cordon to protect Muslim countrymen when they bowed toward Mecca for midday prayers. The scene became a powerful representation of the Egyptian Revolution. Above the vast sea of heads that formed a series of concentric ripples radiating outward from the central square, the crowd lifted two Egyptian men, their arms up in the air, one holding a Quran and the other a Christian cross. "We're all together in this boat," they chanted. Soon the Muslim crescent embracing the Christian cross, a symbol of the 1919 Egyptian Revolution for independence from the British Crown, was back on wall graffiti, flags, and signs at Tahrir Square. On February 11, 2011, after eighteen days of demonstrations, President Mubarak resigned.

I went to Cairo to follow Luiz and Gis's new and even more ambitious mission in the Muslim world. Luiz showed me a list of three hundred Brazilian missionaries working in the Middle East and Asia whom the veteran couple planned to visit. The list had been put together by American evangelist Ted Limpic, who along with Luis Bush was one of the most prominent catalysts of missions from Latin America to the world. Ted and Claudia, his wife, had served as missionaries in Brazil for twenty-two years, during which their influence extended to the entire region. As a researcher of Christian missions, Limpic accepted an invitation from the Lausanne Committee for World Evangelization to help map and organize the embryonic mission movement of Latin American evangelicals. The couple moved to Brazil, and immediately got involved in helping organize the first Ibero-American Missionary Congress, designed by Luis Bush. That was in the late eighties and the Lausanne Committee, according to Ted Limpic, already had in mind that Brazil "could and should be a missionary-sending country."

In 2005, Ted used his vast network of contacts in Latin America to conduct research which indicated that the number of Latin American missionaries in general, and Brazilians in particular, was growing fast. But they weren't staying in the field long. Even those who were supported financially were often neglected pastorally, his research found. After decades recruiting, training, and sending Brazilians as missionaries to the "least reached peoples" in the world, the Limpics moved to Malaga, in southern Spain. From there they began providing pastoral care for Latin American missionaries serving across the Muslim world.

"Our idea is to assist them with whatever they need," S. P. Luiz told me. He and his wife were soon to join the ministry. The decision had been taken following a meeting with the Limpics during the congress in Águas de Lindoia. The missionary couple planned to stay in Brazil only until the family's visas to Europe were issued. A Baptist church in Scotland, the same one that had hosted Luiz and Gis while they were studying English before moving to Afghanistan, had offered them housing and a plot of land where the couple planned to build a guesthouse for missionaries coming in and out of Muslim countries. The place would serve as a base for the couple, who would visit Brazilian missionaries in fields across the Middle East and Asia. Egypt was to be their first destination as part of the new mission endeavor, and I decided to follow them.

The fourth anniversary of the Egyptian Revolution was approaching, but there was no reason to celebrate. The revolution had died after a short-lived affair with democracy, and the high spirits of the Arab Spring had gone from enthusiasm and hope to resignation and despair. American warplanes were back in Iraq and had started bombing parts of Syria on a campaign against Al-Qaeda-affiliated groups—new networks of jihadists that had emerged from the ruins of the civil wars in those countries.

Yet, the evangelical missionaries in Egypt had a different perception of the situation. "The Arab Spring had a great impact on the Church in Egypt. As tragic as it was, we saw God's hands on it," Muna's husband, Sobhy, said while driving around an empty Tahrir Square after picking us up at the airport. The uprising, he argued, forced Egyptian evangelicals, who constituted an isolated minority within the Christian minority in the Arab country, out of the church walls and into the streets. "They went back to the foundational Christian principles: engaging society, loving their neighbors, and growing the church," Sobhy said. Luiz agreed: "I believe God is working to dethrone rulers and destroy old structures. Walls and traditions are falling."

Moheb Milad, a thirty-seven-year-old youth leader at Kasr El Dobara, told me enthusiastically how he had led groups of young Protestant evangelicals into Tahrir Square during the electrifying first three weeks of the Egyptian Revolution until the fall of Mubarak. "We would go out with the guitar and praise God for thirty minutes," he said. The public worship was described by the general media as a "Coptic mass," but, as anthropologist Anthony Shenoda noted, it was instead a pure Protestant evangelical liturgy. The public worship services at Tahrir Square were an extremely rare televised display of Christian faith.

Days after the fall of Mubarak, Kasr el Dobara hosted a memorial service for the "Martyrs of the Revolution." Islam Lotfi, a then thirty-three-year-old lawyer and member of the Muslim Brotherhood, gave the main address to the sound of hymns and clapping hands: a youth leader of Egypt's outlawed Islamist Muslim Brotherhood, talking tolerance to a congregation of warmly applauding Christians. The service—noisy with prayers, hymns, taped video tributes to the young protesters, and wails from the pews—commemorated the Muslim and Christian young people killed in the uprising. When pro-government forces attacked, "Muslims stood to protect the Christians at prayer," Lotfi said, describing lines of young men holding rocks that had formed at each faith's time of worship. "And then Christians stood to protect the Muslims."

This kind of public involvement brought significant media coverage to what many leaders and congregants now call "the Tahrir Church." It also shaped how Kasr el Dobara members saw their role in this revolutionary moment in Cairo.

Muna and Sobhy Abdelmassih, who go by their Arab nicknames for safety reasons, offered to host Luiz, Gis, and me at their home in southern Cairo. Their three teenage children, nicknamed Hanna, Moses, and Joseph, and a friendly golden retriever welcomed us at the house. A gigantic crucifix reading "Jesus" hung on the wall over a big-screen TV in the living room, a showy reminder of our hosts' higher purpose in the country.

Muna and Sobhy had first heard of Luiz and Gis in Afghanistan years before. Another Brazilian missionary and fellow of Barros's house church had asked Muna and Sobhy if they could host a couple serving along with Luiz and Gis in Kabul. That couple needed a break from the field and a place abroad to renew their Afghan visas. Soon after, Sobhy and Muna received a visit from Ted and Claudia Limpic. In 2008, Ted was still trying to identify and locate Latin American missionaries in the field and asked Sobhy if he knew others like him. "Oh! So many. So many!" Sobhy answered. "I know Brazilian missionaries serving even in Afghanistan!" The American mission leaders soon landed in Kabul to meet Luiz and Gis, and began visiting the couple every year. "[Luiz] opened his heart to Ted about the need to provide pastoral care for missionaries in the field, and that was exactly what Ted was starting to do, and he thought it would be fantastic to have someone with so much field experience working with him," Sobhy said.

The evening after we arrived in Cairo, Sobhy and Muna hosted fellow countrymen serving as missionaries in Egypt for worship and Brazilian-style barbecue to welcome Luiz and Gis. They were from various denominations and parts of Brazil, except for one American accompanying his Brazilian missionary wife and holding the couple's newborn baby while she prayed vigorously. Someone brought a guitar and began playing a song by Brazilian Baptist leader Ana Paula Valadão, a sponsor and enthusiast of missions, the founder and pastor of the Florida-based Before the Throne Church, and a gospel singer with some twenty-five recorded albums that have sold over fifteen million copies. The missionaries sang along enthusiastically. Some, like Gis, cried aloud in adoration while Luiz spoke in tongues and wept.

"I was asked to share a few words with you today," Luiz started after the worship. "I want to honor your lives for your dedication, service to the Lord, and commitment. You have taken an incredible step toward the Lord that I believe everyone should take," he said, breaking into tears. In the following days, Luiz and Gis visited a dozen Brazilian missionaries stationed in Egypt.

Egypt is one of the earliest centers of Christianity. Here, the Apostle Mark, the Evangelist, is believed to have converted the first Greeks and Jews. He is celebrated as the founder of the Church of Alexandria, where a distinct type of Christianity developed, leading to a schism with Rome that established the Coptic Orthodox Church. At the time, 80 percent of Egyptians adhered to Christianity. The Christian population began to decline during the seventh-century Muslim conquest, and by the ninth century, Christians ceased to be a majority.

Christian missionaries from the West began arriving in Egypt only a millennium later. In 1852, after visiting the country, J. G. Paulding of the Associate Reformed Presbyterian Church mission in Damascus, Syria, wrote to leaders of his American church in Pennsylvania, describing Egypt as an open field for Christian mission. The first American missionaries arrived shortly after, and established the Evangelical Church of Egypt, also called the Synod of the Nile, as a mission of the American Presbyterian Church. They founded the country's first primary schools for girls; higher educational institutions, such as the American University; as well as hospitals and orphanages. They started the Evangelical Theological Seminary of Cairo in a houseboat that sailed up and down the Nile from Aswan to Cairo. Students on board took classes in the mornings and returned to the riverside communities to preach the gospel in the evening. These earlier missionaries preached primarily among Copts.

Nevertheless, their massive presence didn't go unnoticed by Islamist groups like the Muslim Brotherhood, which emerged in 1928 out of a revivalist movement following the collapse of the Ottoman Empire. Historian Beth Baron argues that the formation of the Islamist group was a reaction to the growing presence of Christian missionaries in Egypt at the time. Muslim nationalists began denouncing the missionaries for attempting to convert Muslim youths. Then, in 1933, a fifteen-year-old Muslim girl refused to stand for the headmaster of a Christian school in Port Said, and it became a watershed moment.

Turkiyya Hasan attended a Christian school associated with the orphanage run by foreign missionaries of which she was a resident. Her defiant behavior was punished with beatings. The local police learned about it, and the news spread as proof of Western missionaries' misdeeds toward Muslims, leading to calls for the government to restrain Christian missions in the country.

Ultimately, the leadership of all Christian missionary enterprises was transferred to the hands of native Muslims. The Muslim Brotherhood seized this opportunity to start building their own community-based networks, which later proved to be a valuable political asset. As of the 2012 presidential elections, the Brotherhood ran 1,200 civil societies and branches in about 6,000 mosques, 20 hospitals, and 20 Egyptian NGOs that provided essential social services to the poor and marginalized.

When the January 25 protests began at Tahrir Square, Copts were mourning the brutal death of twenty-three worshippers from a suicide bomb at an Alexandria church's New Year service. The church's leadership was well aware of the alliances, at times controversial, that its survival depended on. Fearing that regime change could result in increased persecution of Christians if Islamists came to power, the Copt Patriarch Father Shenouda publicly declared support for Hosni Mubarak.

Days after the Copt Patriarch announced his position, some fifty evangelical leaders in Egypt signed a public statement supporting the uprising. Youth groups from Kasr El Dobara Evangelical Church, which is situated in Tahrir Square and is the largest Protestant evangelical church in the Middle East, organized trash pickup and food distribution. The leadership allowed their property to be used for strategy meetings for protest organizers. Others joined the protesters.

On October 27, 2011, the military attacked a Coptic protest, killing twenty-seven Coptic Christians, many of them run over by military tanks. The incident prompted a new wave of protests, calling for the military to surrender power to an interim civilian government. The army had postponed the handover until after the presidential election, while writing a set of rules that would grant the armed forces permanent powers under the new Constitution. The amendments were withdrawn, but a few hundred protesters camped at Tahrir. An attempt to forcibly evacuate the Square instead drew thousands of Egyptians into the streets, and violent clashes erupted.

Back in Cairo, Sobhy received a call from a friend and leader from Kasr El Dobara: *We are losing many lives*. When Sobhy had first arrived with his family in Egypt, they had no money except for basic living expenses paid by their Baptist church in Brazil, spoke no Arabic, and knew nothing about the country. For the first three years, he walked every corner of Greater Cairo, praying in silence. His wanderings brought him fame among the evangelicals in Egypt, because he knew every inch of its vast capital.

That night, Sobhy walked through clouds of tear gas, bringing boxes of equipment to the church. "The wounded arrived with disfigured faces; dozens of them," Sobhy recalled. The Egyptian police were brutally beating the protesters.

Sobhy was welcomed at the church by a Muslim doctor who had joined the evangelicals in attending to the injured from Tahrir Square. Throughout the night, more and more evangelical, Christian Orthodox, and Muslim people arrived at the church and volunteered at its improvised field hospital. That, too, became a powerful symbol of the spirit of the revolution and interfaith unity for freedom and democracy, as well as of Christian benevolence—or so the leaders of Kasr El Dobara hoped.

On November 28, Egyptians went to the polls for the first free parliamentary elections in the country's history. Islamist parties took over 70 percent of the seats. The following year, the Muslim Brotherhood's Mohamed Morsi won the elections, becoming the first democratically elected president in the history of Egypt and the first Islamist to head the country.

While many pro-democracy activists were disappointed, among Protestant evangelicals, the mood was somewhat different. "We have two realities in Egypt: the Muslim Brotherhood taking authority and Muslims coming to the church like you have never seen before," Milad, the youth leader at Kasr el Dobara, told me just four months after Morsi's election. "We are in a spiritual moment," he added. "[Muslims] are coming to the church every day."

The new faces arriving at the churches were primarily young, and many saw the hands of Luis Bush pushing them. Beginning in 2009, a Brazilian pastor named Odijon Ribeiro came to Egypt as Bush's envoy to share a "new vision" from the evangelical strategist: the 4/14 Movement. It further sharpened the focus of Christian missions to reach children aged four to fourteen inside the 10/40 Window. An astonishing 70 percent of all children at that age lived inside the 10/40 Window, and evangelicals knew their survival and future depended on the next generation.

The vision led to the 4/14 Window Middle East conference, in which 230 Christian leaders came from all around the Arab world committed to organizing "the biggest children's conference that Egypt had ever seen." At the meeting, Luis Bush promised: "From Egypt will come a revival to the world."

The conference happened amid new clashes. Egyptians were back on the streets in a new wave of protests, this time against Morsi. The protests culminated with the president's defense minister, General Abdel Fattah El-Sisi, taking power in a coup. The government's security forces stormed two camps in Cairo occupied by supporters of the ousted Morsi, killing hundreds of Muslims. It was the worst mass killing in Egyptian history and the end of Egypt's Revolution.

The brutality by the military government against fellow Muslims also unleashed a wave of violence against Christians in the country. Dozens of churches and monasteries were torched, including the 1,600-year-old monastery of the Virgin Mary. Christian homes, schools, and shops were attacked. In the southern province of Minya, mobs carrying machetes and firearms took control of the village of Delga, killing those who resisted and forcing scores of families to flee the town. Episodes of interfaith strife erupted, often flaring over conversions, family disputes, and the construction of churches.

After teaching himself Arabic by taking free online courses and talking to people on the streets of Cairo, Sobhy established a firm that designed and launched social responsibility programs for private companies in Egypt. Sobhy also ran the programs, which included soccer coaching, arts, and other activities offered to street children and Muslim families in the poorest neighborhoods in greater Cairo.

That guaranteed Sobhy and other Brazilian missionaries who came to work with him both the respect of local elites and access to vulnerable Muslims, all with funding from his clients in the private sector. "As a foreign businessman, I have access to [Muslim] families that Egyptian Christians don't and to places where the native Christians can't go," Sobhy told me.

Christian missionaries under his supervision in Egypt did not openly preach the gospel among the Muslims who attended; like Luiz and Gis at the school and pizza-delivery business in Afghanistan, Sobhy forbade his team to talk about religion during business hours. They were also extra careful not to use words such as *mission* or *missionary*, using slang to refer to them instead. (For safety reasons, they asked me not to reveal the slang terms they used.)

The Brazilian missionaries used encrypted messaging and email services to communicate with each other. They never talked about religion or proselytizing on the phone. They didn't use their real names. Most kept away from social media. Sobhy was obsessed with online spies and scammers, and he would spend an hour every night before sleeping tracing any vestiges of the family online. The Brazilian missionaries were also vigilant about their own behavior, both in how they related to and communicated with Muslims and how they behaved in public. Like S. P. Luiz and Gis in Afghanistan, the idea was to show "the love of Christ" by being role models as professionals, friends, husband and wife, father and mother, and by exposing the family "blessings"—a good marriage, educated children, a prosperous business, and so on.

One fellow countryman and mission leader in Egypt, Dagnaldo Pinheiro Gomes, had recently been arrested on a visit to the Pyramids with a group of tourists when authorities checked his car for bombs and found instead Bibles in Arabic.

One Egyptian, a Coptic Orthodox believer who had converted to evangelical Christianity and worked with Sobhy and Muna, was arrested and questioned after another Brazilian missionary was caught photographing Egyptian soldiers in the middle of the uprising. In the camera, the authorities found suspicious photographs of Christian activities, and they pressured the Egyptian convert to denounce them. He claimed that he had been hired as a driver and denied knowing them. After his release, a mission leader in Egypt sent him to Brazil for two months so he could disappear for a while. While there, he completed a forty-five-day course and was certified as an international soccer coach. Back in Egypt, he began preaching to three teenage Muslim players who attended the soccer training program, and they became his first disciples. "I now work converting Muslims," he said.

One Sunday, he took me to Kasr El Dobara. We arrived just before the service. The church pews were half full. The church had white walls and tall stained-glass windows depicting New Testament stories of Jesus. Except for the Egyptian flag behind the pulpit, nothing in the building indicated that we were at a church in Cairo. The service resembled any US megachurch, with a band onstage, loud music, lyrics projected on the wall, passionate preaching, and holy-spirited worshippers shouting joyfully. Kasr El Dobara maintained the characteristics embodied in US Evangelicism: a confessional and personal faith, a high view of the authority of Scripture, a non-rigid church hierarchy, a strong belief in supernatural healing and in the spiritual gift of speaking in tongues—and, more recently, a priority to Evangelism and social services among non-Christians.

"We are living in a moment of freedom. The [Egyptian] revolution started with young people asking for freedom. So, oddly enough, we are enjoying certain freedom to preach the gospel," Sobhy said. "We always had that tension in the air and fear that someone could be listening to our conversations. The tensions disappeared a little bit. In some places, we can sit down and converse like we're having here. And many, many are accepting Jesus. There are a lot of people. . . . And we are short of workers," he said. "The doors are open."

Another Brazilian missionary in Egypt told me he was supporting a group of twenty-five young Egyptian evangelical Christians dedicated to preaching the gospel to Muslims. "They are now teaching seventy-five disciples who are new converts," he told me. "After the revolution, Muslims opened up for the gospel, and they are living the golden age of His ministry. In these past years, there has been more of this than in the previous thousand years."

To Protestant evangelicals in Egypt, the Arab Spring was God's answer to their long-standing prayers.

On November 28, 2014, just a few days after I left Cairo, the Salafi Front called on Egyptians to take to the streets holding copies of the Quran and demand the restoration of Egypt's "[Islamic] identity and Sharia Law." They called it the Red Friday Million-Man March, and promised "the start of an Islamic revolution to topple the military regime and uphold the word of God in Egypt."

The Islamist call to restore Egypt's "Islamic identity" failed. Most Egyptians viewed violent Islam as more dangerous than the country's military. Soon after, militants in the Sinai pledged loyalty to the Islamic State of Iraq and Syria. Few people had heard of ISIS before that June, when the armed group crossed the border from Syria into northern Iraq, taking control of Mosul, Iraq's second-largest city. In February the next year, ISIS uploaded one of its many gruesome videos, "A Message in Blood Written to the Nation of the Cross," showing the beheadings of twenty-one migrant workers in Libya. All but one of the victims were Coptic Christians from Egypt.

In one of our last days in Egypt, Luiz asked me if I remembered him telling me about a dream he had many years ago. It was of clouds of fire in the sky and scores of people running away in different directions. "I see this massive diaspora arriving at the shores of Europe, coming from the Middle East, and I think that perhaps this might be something created by God. I believe God is taking people from here and putting them there," he had said. I didn't immediately grasp the connection Luiz was trying to make. "Don't you see? We no longer need to go to Afghanistan to evangelize Muslims; there are millions of Afghans in Europe now and hundreds of thousands more in the United States, in Brazil . . . everywhere! Instead of paying attention to what God is doing so we can work with these people, Christians are busy clinging to old structures and traditions," Luiz said. "But I've been asking myself: What if God is moving people?"

What If God Is Moving People?

"Jesus Loves You," read the T-shirt of a Christian aid worker welcoming refugees with thermal fleece blankets and prayers on the Greek island of Lesbos. In October of 2015, more than ten thousand men, women, and children arrived at the island daily, crossing on fragile boats from Turkey. That year, global mass displacement reached a record high of 65.3 million people. Some 21.3 million of them were refugees, of which Syrians were the largest group, followed by Afghans. But Tamana Hedayat never made it.

I had met Tamana three years earlier, when she taught Dari to foreign missionaries at the school Gis founded and directed in Kabul. Fatema, who with her husband, Henrique, took over the mission in Afghanistan, had been teaching the Bible to Tamana, after the Afghan teacher told her of a dream she had with a "bearded man" involved in a bright aura. Fatema was convinced Tamana had a vision of Jesus. But the situation in Afghanistan had worsened dramatically since I last saw Tamana. The international troop withdrawal in 2014 had failed to achieve its objectives, and the Taliban was making gains. Afghans working for foreigners had become targets of frequent attacks, and Tamana now dreamed of Europe.

Fatema had unsuccessfully tried to raise funds from church members to help Afghan converts get out of the country. In the summer of 2015, Tamana learned that she was pregnant, and raising a child in Afghanistan terrified her. So she decided she could wait no longer. By then, more than 2.5 million Afghans had left the country and sought asylum abroad. Tamana's family sold all their belongings to pay smugglers to take them by land to Turkey. But after an epic fifty-seven-day journey that included two failed attempts to reach Bulgaria, Europe felt like a mirage in the desert. European countries had deployed soldiers at their borders, and built walls and miles-long fences to stop the influx of asylum seekers. The increased security on land pushed hundreds of thousands of refugees into the troubled waters of the Mediterranean and Aegean Seas. At least 2,500 people died that summer attempting to make the sea crossing to safety in Europe. Tamana was terrified of the sea; her whole family was. Afghanistan is a landlocked country, and they had never seen the sea. Fatema called Tamana and begged her to give up the plan.

At a clinic in a Turkish refugee camp, Tamana was informed that she was expecting a girl. She named her daughter Nihan, after the protagonist of the series *Endless Love* that had just made its debut on Turkish TV. On the night of October 16, 2015, the family arrived in the district of Ayvalik in the Çanakkale Province of northwestern Turkey. The boat waiting for them wasn't as big as the smuggler had said, but the crossing point was the closest to Lesbos. For Tamana and her family, it meant the future was just a short distance away.

Sulaiman, Tamana's husband, counted more than forty people crammed on board the old, small fishing boat. At 7:45 p.m., the pilot started the engine and turned the bow toward Lesbos. Then, after a few minutes, he jumped in the water and disappeared into the darkness. One common practice among smugglers was to send the boats out with only enough fuel to enter neighboring waters, where if they were lucky, local authorities would rescue the passengers. A Syrian man volunteered to take control of the boat. The waves became bigger and bigger and pummeled the boat from all sides. After about an hour, the group realized they had lost the way. As the man maneuvered, trying to change directions, a strong wave broke the boat into two pieces.

The next day, the Turkish state-run Anadolu news agency reported that a boat had sunk off its shores with forty-eight Syrians and Afghans on board. The coast guard had rescued twenty-three of them. Among the survivors who appeared on TV, Fatema recognized Tamana's younger brother and his wife. They seemed agitated and exhausted, their eyes swollen. Some cried aloud. A separate vessel brought ashore the dead bodies of twelve migrants, including four children and a baby. Among them were Tamana's mother, father, and younger sister.

Tamana's brother recognized the bodies. He later found Tamana's husband, Sulaiman, who had survived and been taken to a camp, but his sister remained missing after days. So, he returned to Kabul, bringing the bodies of his family to be buried in their beloved homeland. Sulaiman stayed in Turkey to search for Tamana.

Luiz, Gis, Henrique, and Fatema reached out to missionaries serving among refugees in Turkey. A Brazilian family living in Istanbul found Sulaiman crammed with a dozen other Afghans in a shaggy hotel room arranged by a smuggler, waiting to make another attempt to cross the sea to Greece. Sulaiman did not want to go anywhere. He had promised himself he would only leave Turkey with Tamana, so the Christian family brought him home to Istanbul.

I spoke to Sulaiman days later. He had recurring nightmares, and when I spoke to him, he would repeatedly recall the scene of the shipwreck. He had insistently called for Tamana but couldn't see her or anyone else in the dark. He stayed in the water for some three hours, the coast guard later told him, before being rescued. He almost immediately began a desperate search for his pregnant wife, which involved the entire global church. A detailed description of Tamana's physical features, deep black hair, and bright green eyes, with pictures of her in Afghanistan and during the journey, was printed and distributed across the shores of Greece and Turkey, and circulated to Christians across the globe.

During his search, Sulaiman remained with the Brazilian family. They offered him practical and emotional support as well as prayers, and he would accompany them to all church services and events. They spent Christmas and Easter together. But the days became weeks, which became months. After a year living in Istanbul, without any hope of being granted asylum or finding Tamana, Sulaiman returned to Afghanistan and to Islam. Tamana remains missing; she was twenty-five and was five months pregnant.

In the fall of 2015, I flew to northern Iraq and crossed the Tigris River into northeast Syria. I wanted to understand what role religion played in the dynamics of the conflicts causing an exodus of biblical proportion from the Middle East, the cradle of Christianity, radiating in waves as far as Europe and the United States.

Along the road from Erbil to the border crossing via Dohuk, large camps for Syrian refugees and internally displaced Iraqis stretched out of sight. These tents sheltered mostly Christian and Yazidi peoples expelled from their ancient homelands. Thousands more were leaving Syria. The small, rusty metal boat I crossed in reached the harbor of Faysh Khabur, on the Iraqi side, packed with large families carrying endless bags, and returned empty back into Syria. Across the Tigris River, I was welcomed in Syrian territory by Kurdish fighters who escorted me to a nearby command post to be screened and identified—and then left me and the photographer on our own.

On the road to Amuda, I passed oil fields, photos of "martyred" men and women hanging from poles, and ancient Christian villages, now emptied. I crossed Qamishli, originally a Christian town named Bet Zalin (it translates as "House of Reeds"), founded by survivors of the Assyrian genocide in the early twentieth century.

Before the pro-democracy protests turned into a bloody civil war in Syria, some forty thousand Christians remained in Qamishli, but they had almost vanished by the time I reached the town. The town had become the de facto capital of the Kurdish-controlled territory, with its downtown secured by the Syrian Army. Two gigantic posters of Syrian president Bashar al-Assad watched us from a distance.

Christians in Syria had traditionally supported the Assad regime, less out of conviction than as a means of survival. Christians never enjoyed equal rights with the majority-Muslim Syrian citizens under the Assad regime, but at least they were a tolerated minority. Just as in Egypt, radical Islamists posed an existential threat to Christians, but they weren't the only problem. The Kurds saw the war as an opportunity to build a long-desired independent state in the majority-Kurdish stretch of land in northern Syria bordering Turkey. Busy fighting many factions, Assad unofficially allowed the Kurds to secure the land as long as they didn't fight his regime. In Al-Hasakah province, where Qamishli is located, Christians accused the Kurds of grabbing properties as they pushed rebels—and eventually Christian neighbors—out of these lands.

In fact, Christians in Al-Hasakah had formed a militia of their own, the Syriac Military Council, with two thousand Assyrian, Syriac, and Chaldean Christian fighters. I hoped to interview them. The only place to find soldiers was at the trenches opposing the Islamic State. So I followed two Kurdish soldiers to a logistics post in the center of Al-Hasakah supplying the fighters on the front lines.

Inside, I recognized a Christian Assyrian fighter based on how he greeted me. He was from Tell Shamiram, a small village inhabited by Christians. Just before dawn, on February 23, 2015, heavily armed ISIS fighters had descended on Tell Shamiram and dozens of other Christian villages in the region, taking hundreds hostage. Ninety residents of the soldier's hometown, primarily elders, were abducted, including his parents. So he joined the militias fighting ISIS. By March of that year, the village had been completely emptied. A few abductees from nearby villages, such as Tell Tamer, were freed in exchange for exorbitant ransoms. But the Christian soldier had just learned that his father had been executed, and he had no news of his mother.

The attack came months after ISIS swept through Sinjar in northern Iraq, leading to the genocide of the Yazidis. Many who managed to escape fled across the Tigris to Hasakah and Qamishli in Syria. Then ISIS attacked these towns.

That was all the Christian Assyrian soldier could tell me before our conversation was interrupted by the deafening dry thud of a massive explosion. We fell to the floor. A dense, dark cloud shot through the window by which we were sitting and engulfed us in dust, shattered glass, and fragments of twisted steel. We fell to the floor with the strong impact of the explosion. The soldier quickly stood up, emerging from the debris, and ran toward the front of the gate, firing an old Kalashnikov. More gunfire broke out, signaling that the Islamic State combatants were near, placing us in a state of panic.

I crawled through the debris-covered floor to one of the tall columns holding up the roof, in case a second explosion brought down the walls. I stayed there for three hours while an intense gunfight raged outside. When the guns were silenced, Kurdish fighters wrapped the scattered bodies in large rugs and put them on the back of a pickup truck before evacuating the partially collapsed building.

The explosion had opened a massive crater by the gate where a guard, now dead, had checked our documents just a few hours before. Ruin and debris extended in every direction. We found our rented van with shattered glass windows and twisted doors that failed to close, but the engine still worked. Back in Amuda, the mood was tense. A hollow-eyed Kurdish commander in ragtag uniform counted one hundred people dead, most of them civilians, in multiple bomb attacks across the region that day.

Just weeks before I traveled to Syria, Al-Hasakah had been partially liberated by the Kurdish and Assyrian militias. But ISIS had left behind tons of explosives and suicide bombers who were ready to die in the name of the Islamic State.

Many evangelicals in the West pleaded for Christians to be evacuated to safety out of Iraq and Syria. But that would mean the jihadists had won, successfully pushing Christians out of their ancient homelands.

Amid this ISIS offensive, Brazilian pastor Homero Azis traveled from his base in Jordan to northern Iraq, where he joined a priest of the Assyrian Church of the East on a trip to retrace the path of Iraqi Christians fleeing ISIS.

The missionary was escorted by the Nineveh Plain Protection Units, a militia formed early in 2015 by Iraqi Christians, many forced to leave their homes by jihadists. The semi-autonomous Kurdish government in northern Iraq forbade Christians to bear arms. But with ISIS's advance, permission was granted as long as the Christian militia operated under the command of the Peshmerga, the Kurdish forces in northern Iraq.

When Azis first went to Telskuf, ISIS was just around the corner. The jihadists still controlled Mosul and most nearby Christian villages. "It was the most dangerous trip I undertook," Azis said. Nevertheless, when I met Azis in Jordan in January 2018, he had returned to Iraq seven times and was preparing for another trip there. "We are trying to rapidly restore ministries and to prepare for the families to return as soon as these areas are liberated, because Muslims are taking Christians' homes as they advance against ISIS," Azis told me. "So these neighborhoods could be Islamicized, and we are trying to avoid that."

Sectarianism was evident in Iraq. Back across the Tigris River, at a military post in Makhmour, a Peshmerga commander showed me the map that began to emerge from the conflicts. It had the unofficial borders of what he named Kurdistan, Jihadistan, and Shiastan, referring to the territories dominated by Kurdish militias in the north, the Islamic State in the majority-Sunni Arab central corridor, and Shia Arab rebels in the south. It wasn't that Christians had no safe place in the new Iraq—they had no place at all.

I met Azis through Luiz and Gis, who had traveled to Jordan as part of their new mission, supporting Brazilian missionaries serving among Muslims in the Middle East and Asia. Azis's ministry and mission in Jordan had grown into a multi-service enterprise, with a clinic, a gym, a community center, a kindergarten, a school, and programs offering microcredit, carpentry, and soccer coaching to refugees, mostly Muslims. Additional Brazilian missionaries had been sent to help Azis. Among them was a lawyer who had just started providing legal advice for refugees at higher risk of persecution or facing life threats to seek asylum in the United States and Europe. While they waited for a visa, they were sheltered at an underground safe house maintained by Azis's Al-Rahwa mission.

The Missão em Apoio à Igreja Sofredora, an organization started by a former Brazilian missionary, paid the Azis family's basic living expenses. Less than one-fifth of the mission's monthly costs of $14,000 were covered with funding from US evangelical churches and organizations. The rest were covered by rents from a guesthouse Azis and his wife had opened to receive aspiring missionaries. Al-Rahwa Ministry had thirty-two full-time Christian workers. Most of them were Arab refugees, "born again" evangelicals converted from either the Assyrian Church of the East or from Islam.

One of them was Yaqub, an Iraqi refugee, and former devoted Muslim. Yaqub had survived countless attempts on his life. Those included being kidnapped at seventeen by Shia militiamen who tortured him and threatened to cut his body into pieces to feed to dogs. His father, a former military officer under Saddam Hussein, listened to his son's pleas on the other side of the phone line for five days, until the family sold their house and car, and paid the criminals $30,000 to free Yaqub. Yaqub's best friend, Hassan, who was also kidnapped, was not so lucky, for his father did not have the money to pay for the boy's life.

Life had become unbearable in Baghdad. Al-Qaeda militants offered protection to families in exchange for the men in the house joining their ranks. Yaqub had refused, and was labeled an infidel, becoming a target of Sunni militiamen—despite himself being a devoted Sunni Muslim. Yaqub had read in the Quran that being a good Muslim would prevent him from going to hell—except that he was already living in hell. So the family crossed the border into Jordan.

Days before we met, Yaqub had found a death threat slipped under the door of his temporary home in a suburb of Amman. Now twenty-seven and a born-again evangelical Christian, Yaqub was no longer scared, for he believed he would be protected by Jesus. He had first learned about Christianity from the evangelicals assisting Iraqi and Syrian refugees in Jordan, and he was now helping Azis spread the gospel among fellow Muslims. "I know exactly what Muslims believe," he told me.

Sitting next to us was another Christian Iraqi, a dentist and former employee of Franklin Graham's Samaritan's Purse, who had escaped from Mosul. "When I worked for Samaritan's Purse, scores converted to Christianity. Some conversions are not real. When aid leaves, they are back in the mosques," he told me. But some conversions were real. "The only reason Muslims are converting to Christianity, I mean, *really* converting, is not aid; it is ISIS."

In fact, despite the international pleas from Christians trapped by ISIS in Iraq and Syria, Muslims were the most affected by these wars. Most civilians were slaughtered by fellow Muslim jihadists. "ISIS is the most important cause for people to leave [their countries and Islam]. Because they realized that the so-called Islamic State was targeting Muslims. People were so disappointed with the violent side of their religion that they either turned to another religion or simply became nonbelievers. They stopped believing even in God," he said. "Muslims and Christians were living together in Iraq until the United States brought us their democracy of terrorism. All the problems [Muslim] people have is with the Americans. But when you say 'Brazilian,' they just think: 'Football!'"

Looking back, Azis believed 9/11 had been a plan designed and executed by Al-Qaeda to raise Muslims for jihad and for global terrorism. "But, parallel to such demonic strategy, we see that God is using this moment in a very special way to awaken the Muslim world spiritually," he said. I ask what he means by God using this moment. "God is moving all these people, I have no doubt. And I feel I'm harvesting from this awakening," he said. "Early Western missionaries, American and British, would be here for twenty years without touching one life. I, alone, already baptized fourteen—in Jordan only."

In videos shared with me by Zeyad Zaid, the Iraqi convert who had been injured in an ambush while working with the US Army through a contractor back in his country, he appears fully recovered from his leg injuries and walking barefoot into the river Jordan. Enveloped in a white robe, he is guided by Pastor Philip Sahawneh and a short-term American missionary. Each holds one of Zaid's arms; they immerse him in the water, as it goes in the Protestant evangelical tradition. The ritual marks one's conversion, and it can happen at any time in life, but not at birth, like in Catholicism. The believer must be ready to receive "the gift of the Holy Spirit" and commit to a "new life in Jesus Christ." The drowning symbolizes the death of sins. By emerging from the water, one is "born again."

At the site of Jesus's baptism, the river Jordan flows through the Jordan Rift Valley and the Sea of Galilee (Lake Kinneret, in the Old Testament). It is believed that Jesus recruited his Apostles from the lakeside villages, and Christianity started spreading. Zaid repeated the ritual, this time led into the river by Homero Azis. It was not a second baptism but a representation of a scene described in Acts 19, where Paul placed his hands on a group of disciples, and "the Holy Spirit came upon them, and they spoke in tongues and prophesied." Wearing the same white robe, with Azis's hands upon him, Zaid vowed to fulfill the Great Commission. "I promised to use my testimony to spread His name," Zaid said. "I wanted to serve among refugees like me."

The Last Frontier

In February 2016, Zaid arrived in the United States under a Special Immigration Visa—a status granted to individuals who aided the American government in Afghanistan or Iraq. Three years before, he had been welcomed at the Jordanian border by Azis's Al-Rahwa mission, who introduced him to American short-term missionaries from the Arabic Church in Anaheim, California. The church offered to sponsor Zaid's visa, and that's how he found himself in Southern California.

In America, Zaid's time is divided between his formal job repairing the glass of luxury cars—"Lamborghini, Bentley, Rolls-Royce, Porsche"—and serving the church. "Many Muslims come to our church," he told me. "Sometimes we go to the mall to give Bibles to the Muslims, to tell them about Jesus. Our church is very active." On weekends, Zaid worked at the Arabic Church services as a cameraman, and eventually he began producing evangelical videos in Arabic to support US missionary efforts among Muslims.

The Christian Arabic Church of Anaheim was founded by an Egyptian immigrant, Pastor Nabil Abraham, "on both the pillars of evangelism and discipleship." In 2004, the church began sending its flocks on short trips abroad, during which they'd join missionaries serving among Muslims. Then, as the Arab Spring turned into bloody wars, the church was flooded with refugees and immigrants from multiple Middle Eastern countries, and began providing support to those in need of food, medical care, and help with paperwork. At the peak of the refugee crisis in mid-2015, the church formed teams of Christian doctors, nurses, counselors, Sunday school workers, and others to minister to the thousands of Iraqi and Syrian refugees in Jordan.

In Anaheim, the Arabic Church occupied a building owned by Southern Baptists that they shared with Korean- and Spanish-speaking churches. The second floor was rented to Voice of Refugees, a nonprofit founded by three Christians from Iraq, Kuwait, and Jordan. The team consisted of Muslim converts and traditional Christians who lingered at Los Angeles airport terminals searching for newly arrived refugees. They offered them coffee, a warm welcome, and a ride on a donated van to their new home. The missionary work begins on the way, while stuck in LA traffic, when the missionaries offer the refugees help with finding permanent housing, learning English, applying for jobs, enrolling their children in school, using public transport, navigating American culture, and, of course, gaining "eternity through the gospel."

Southern California is a top destination for refugee resettlement in America. El Cajon, near San Diego, is nearly one-third

Iraqi American. Anaheim is also home to Little Arabia, a concentrated row of halal markets, hookah cafes, and Islamic apparel shops. And the new refugees added to those who arrived before. "In the past, the US sent missionaries to the Middle East," Egyptian pastor Nabil Abraham, who arrived in the US forty years ago, told the Christian biweekly magazine *World* at the height of the refugee crisis. "But, now God is bringing the mission field to us in America."

Then came President Donald Trump.

In his first week in office, Trump signed a burst of executive orders that fulfilled vital campaign promises. One order, signed on January 27, 2017, caused particular turmoil. It suspended immigrants from seven Muslim-majority countries—Iran, Iraq, Libya, Sudan, Yemen, Somalia, and Syria—from entering the United States. Thousands of Iraqis who, like Zaid, had risked their lives to help Americans, were left to their own fate. The US government's proposal was to consider applications based on religious persecution "provided that the religion of the individual is a minority religion in the individual's country of nationality." Given that most refugees came from Muslim-majority countries, the proposal meant Christians would have priority.

The backlash from liberals and Democrats was no surprise. But the fiercest opposition to the Muslim ban came from the least expected group: evangelical leaders, most of whom helped to elect the Republican president in the first place. Over a hundred of these leaders from all fifty states signed an open letter addressed to Trump and Vice President Mike Pence to appeal for the reversal of the so-called Muslim ban. Published as a full-page ad in the *Washington Post*, it stated that churches were "eager to welcome persecuted Christians" but also "vulnerable Muslims and people of other faiths or no faith at all."

Written by World Relief, the humanitarian arm of the powerful National Association of Evangelicals (NAE), the open letter contained the names of primarily conservative evangelicals, some of whom rarely spoke out on political matters. Signatories included Leith Anderson, the president of the NAE, representing more than 45,000 churches from forty denominations in the US; the heads of the Southeastern Baptist Theological Seminary of the Southern Baptist Convention; Wheaton College, which had nurtured several generations of fundamentalists since 1860, and the younger Fuller Theological Seminary; as well as the National Latino Evangelical Coalition (NaLEC), a massive alliance of Hispanic evangelical congregations, faith-based nonprofits, and organizations.

Over three thousand evangelical leaders later added their signatures. In the words of Lynne Hybels, co-founder of the Willow Creek Community megachurch, to the *Washington Post*, "Speaking up for and caring for refugees is more an act of worship and obedience to a God whose Kingdom is global."

In December 2015, Ed Stetzer, the dean of Wheaton College, welcomed a hundred prominent evangelical leaders to develop "a sustainable Christian response" to the refugee crisis. The leaders called on believers to "embrace refugees," vowed to prepare their churches to receive them, and agreed to organize a massive conference to discuss the matter. They called it the GC2 Summit, a reference to the Great Commission and Great Commandment from Jesus to spread the gospel to all nations.

"We unashamedly want people to see the love of Christ in the actions that we manifest (as) we render aid," Frank Page, former President and CEO of the Southern Baptist Convention who participated in the meeting, told *Sojourners*. The Southern Baptist Convention officially approved a resolution encouraging churches and family members "to welcome and adopt refugees into their churches and homes." Other evangelicals formed coalitions such as We Welcome Refugees. Believers prayed for refugees outside the hotel in Washington, DC, where Trump attended the National Prayer Breakfast. Christian students and faculty at the conservative Moody Bible Institute in Chicago rallied in their support.

"We have never had an opportunity as we have right now to reach people who are coming to our shores, in many cases from places we have no access to," Scott Arbeiter, president of World Relief, told *Christianity Today*. "We are closing the doors to the very people we say we want to share the Gospel with." World Relief is one of nine agencies that partner with the federal government to resettle refugees. The year before Trump's executive order, the organization assisted about 11,000 refugees, with the help of a volunteer network of 1,200 churches in the United States. At its peak, in the fall of 2016, World Relief resettled forty-five refugees a day at various locations across America.

For Christian aid organizations, Trump's executive order could be devastating domestically and abroad. A backlash against freedom of religion in the United States could cause widespread diplomatic fallout with the Muslim world, limiting the access for American aid organizations, adding risks to the already perilous lives of workers and underground missionaries in these nations, and preventing them from bringing, in the words of Russel Moore, then the president of the Ethics and Religious Liberty Commission of the Southern Baptist Convention, "humanitarian assistance and the love of the gospel." In a separate letter to Trump, Moore urged the president to "ensure the safety of Americans serving in majority-Muslim countries."

The reasons given by most US evangelical leaders offered yet another explanation for their almost unanimous consensus, with a few exceptions among Trump's fiercest white evangelical loyalists, in opposing the Muslim ban. The war in Syria alone had displaced twelve million people, more than half of whom crossed its borders searching for safety. Though the Islamic State created a massive exodus of Christians, most refugees were Muslims. Together, they made up almost half of the twenty-five million refugees in the entire world. "We believe the refugee resettlement program provides a lifeline to these uniquely vulnerable individuals and a vital opportunity for our churches," read the statement urging President Trump to resume the refugee program, signed by eight Christian leaders of the Evangelical Immigration Table, a broad coalition of evangelical organizations advocating for immigration reform.

Suddenly, millions of Muslims were crossing the borders from hostile territories and war zones into the "free world." Building walls and closing borders was not only in conflict with God's Kingdom but led evangelicals to "miss the opportunity," David Cashin, a Muslim-Christian relations expert and intercultural studies professor at Columbia International University, told *Christianity Today* in 2017. For those trying to win souls, the refugee crisis seemed like a blessing. "This is a moment Christian missionaries to the Muslim world have dreamed about for centuries."

However, the almost unanimous position of evangelical leaders in America against the Muslim ban differed from that of their flocks. Self-identified white evangelicals were twice as likely as Americans overall to support the Muslim ban, the Pew Research Center found. Even among their peers, white evangelicals stood out as the religious group least likely to believe the US is responsible for welcoming refugees. Only 25 percent said America has an obligation to refugees, compared to 63 percent of Black Protestants, most of whom identify as evangelical. According to PRRI, they were also the only religious group in America that would grow more supportive of a Muslim ban over time.

The split reflects a broader contemporary divide among US Protestant evangelicals as they struggle to find their place in America and the world. As American evangelical missionaries ventured around the world from the nineteenth century, they saw themselves increasingly engaged with new churches that were anything but homogeneously white, right-wing, or socially conservative. While issues such as abortion and same-sex marriage still bond evangelicals together worldwide, their opinions differ on other subjects, including racism, social justice, immigration, and politics.

Their encounter was not inconsequential. The explosion and growing assertiveness of Protestant Evangelicalism in the Global South and the debates generated by the encounters between missionaries and local converts and religious leaders from both hemispheres have shaped and continue to transform modern Christianity at home and abroad. In foreign fields, US Protestant evangelicals were forced to take stands on issues ranging from pervasive inequality that many in the developing world saw as a result of neoliberal experiments to US-backed anti-communist military regimes in Latin America; from apartheid in South Africa to the horrific torture at Abu Ghraib; and, on controversial domestic issues, from slavery to immigration policy, as they journeyed globally to expand the Kingdom of God—a Kingdom with no walls, where all are equal before God.

Such biblical global vision was mainly at odds with Trump's America-first populist approach to the world, and his election as president widened the divide among Protestant evangelicals in America and abroad. Especially after World War II, US Protestant evangelical leaders became increasingly globalized and came to see themselves as part of a global community that they understood to be God's Kingdom.

"Christians are, in a sense, dual citizens—of the Kingdom and of the nation where they live," Stetzer, of Wheaton College, wrote in his column *The Exchange*. But, he cautioned: "If your church service was driven more by America than by Jesus, I think you need a change."

God's Kingdom, conceived by evangelicals as universal and borderless, sharply contrasted with Trump's isolationist foreign policy. What is more, the diversity inherent to the biblical conception of the Kingdom is what makes North American believers most anxious, especially Trump's most loyal white evangelical supporters, who feared losing the culture war in a pluralistic America.

While US Protestant evangelical leaders became increasingly globalized and engaged with a diverse global religious community, especially since World War II, many in their flocks have not. Their evangelical constituents live in a world deeply divided by national borders and uneven distributions of wealth and power. This split reflects a broader divide among American Protestant evangelicals as they struggle to find their place in America and the world.

Domestically, white Protestant evangelicals remained President Trump's most loyal supporters. They were represented by highly vocal leaders like Franklin Graham, the late media mogul Pat Robertson, and Focus on the Family founder James Dobson, who sided with Trump even through all the scandals of his presidency. But Graham, Robertson, and Dobson speak for a rapidly shrinking faction. They have been criticized, including by fellow evangelicals, for being divisive and politically partisan and blamed for creating a distorted collective consciousness of their peers as a uniformly white conservative "religious-right" Republican voting bloc.

But such a stereotype does not reflect the increasingly diverse US Protestant evangelical community. Though tracking evangelical numbers is as complex as defining them, it is estimated that about a quarter of US adults identify as such. This makes Protestant evangelicals the nation's largest religious group, exceeding Catholics, mainline Protestants, and religiously unaffiliated. Among those self-described evangelicals, 75 percent are white, but their share is decreasing. Half of evangelicals under thirty are nonwhite, and 18 percent are Latinos. Besides being younger than their white religious peers, the new generations are quite different from the church elders: they are more open to same-sex marriage, tend to be environmentalists, and tolerate other religions.

It is also true that church attendance and the Christian share of the population is down in America because the newer generations are leaving the church. Religious "nones" have grown across multiple demographic groups since 2009. On the other hand, Latinos remain one of the nation's fastest-growing ethnic groups, outpacing other groups such as white and Black Americans. And Asian Americans have seen faster population growth than Hispanics. For evangelical leaders, fighting against restrictive immigration policies is a matter of survival.

Mark Chaves, a sociology professor at Duke University, directs a survey of American churches and other places of worship. Diversity within congregations has been growing over the past twenty years. While US churches are still segregated—African Methodist Episcopal Churches are 94 percent Black; Southern Baptists are 85 percent white—multi-racial churches are on the rise. Joel Osteen's Lakewood Church in Houston claims to have, among its 52,000 members, "nearly equal numbers of Caucasian, Hispanic, and African American members."

Church leaders, too, are becoming more diverse. In 2012, the Southern Baptist Convention elected its first Black president. In 2020, Korean American Walter Kim, pastor of the Trinity Presbyterian Church in Charlottesville, Virginia, took the reins of the National Association of Evangelicals. He is the first non-white president in the NAE's seventy-seven years of existence. Born to an immigrant family and raised in Appalachia, Kim said his background would be "an asset to the NAE in a time of polarization" and spoke of the "full notion of the gospel calling us to reconciliation." Johnnie Moore of the United States Commission on International Religious Freedom cheered Kim's election at the time, saying he'd lead "at a time of exponential growth in the global, evangelical movement," a movement facing, in Kim's words, "an identity crisis."

Though the evangelicals' role in electing Trump made headlines, it can be misleading. While eight in ten white evangelical Protestants voted for Trump in 2016, only 35 percent of nonwhite evangelicals did so, and 60 percent voted for the Democratic candidate, Hillary Clinton. "Black evangelicals, Hispanic evangelicals . . . did not vote for Donald Trump. White evangelicals did . . . because they were more white than evangelical," Jim Wallis, a progressive evangelical pastor and former spiritual adviser to Barack Obama, told *New Statesman*. In the 2018 midterm elections, 80 percent of white evangelicals voted for Republicans, and about 76 percent of nonwhite evangelicals voted for Democrats. Meanwhile, many Latinos identify as political independents and became "the ultimate swing vote."

This was evident in the shocking invasion of the Capitol on January 6, 2021, when thousands of mostly white pro-Trump rioters protesting the result of the 2020 US presidential election broke into Congress shouting death threats and carrying weapons, supremacist symbols, and Confederate flags—as well as "Jesus Saves" banners, Christian "flags," and the Holy Bible, while chanting "Christ is king."

That is as important for politics as it is for the future of global Christianity. Ultimately, American Protestant evangelicals will need to choose whether to be citizens of a nation or part of the global, diverse, and borderless Kingdom of God. The Last Frontier of Christendom might well be the doors of the Capitol.

Epilogue

At around 11:00 p.m. on August 14, 2021, in São Paulo, Brazil, my cell phone began beeping frantically with incoming notifications. Senders included Hussain and three former staff members of the Brazilian missionaries' school in Kabul—two teachers and the former director, now married to the taxi driver who drove me around the capital.

The news that the Afghans awoke to that Sunday was predictable but no less shocking: Overnight, the Taliban had taken control of Jalalabad, the country's gateway to the East. There was even talk that its fighters had reached the capital's main entrances. However, there were still American and British troops on the ground there, and it seemed improbable that the Western powers would allow such an embarrassing defeat after twenty years, trillions of dollars, and thousands of lives lost battling the insurgents in America's longest war.

In the following hours, the content of the messages grew increasingly alarming. "The situation is really bad. I'm scared," one WhatsApp message read. "We are locked at home. From the window, we can already see some Taliban fighters roaming on motorbikes." Soon after, Afghan president Ashraf Ghani and his Christian wife, Rula Ghani, fled the country. By the time the Taliban entered the Presidential Palace, an exodus had already begun.

At home on the outskirts of Edinburgh, Luiz received a call from a Christian convert and former employee of his pizza delivery business in Kabul, who broke the news to him and Gis. Luiz immediately contacted Hussain, one of the first Afghan Christians the couple had met sixteen years before in the capital in 2005. Luiz had baptized Hussain's children, and Hussain had been present at the best and the worst times of the Brazilians' missions in Afghanistan. The Afghan convert had survived kidnapping and attempted murder, had been forced to flee Pakistan, where he was a refugee, and had to flee twice again from his own country, Afghanistan—first, to avoid detention and torture after the Noorin TV scandal, and second, after being injured in the Taliban attack that killed Werner Groenewald and his two children. Nevertheless, Hussain remained faithful to Christianity and to Luiz and Gis, with whom he had developed a deep friendship.

Hussain shared with Luiz reports that Taliban fighters were already going door-to-door hunting down Afghan Christians. Luiz and Gis spent the next twenty-two days on the phone, frantically trying to organize a task force to rescue their friends. "Nine families managed to cross the borders to a neighboring country. Others are yet to try making the crossing," Gis wrote to her church in Brazil on WhatsApp. "There are people whose lives are at risk, who have already lost everything, but still haven't been able to leave." Smugglers were overcharging the Afghans to guide them across the border and into neighboring countries, and most of them didn't have the money. "Many don't even have passports or any document," she said.

Luiz and Gis flew to Islamabad, where they rushed to the Brazilian embassy. An attendee told them that the embassy was preparing to receive an influx of Afghan refugees. That afternoon, Gis finally reunited with Hussain and his son-in-law, along with their former school director, her husband, and the couple's two girls.

In Pakistan, most of the Christian refugees had to hide in churches and homes that were arranged by Luiz and Gis. Meanwhile, evangelicals in Brazil lobbied the far-right government of Jair Bolsonaro to authorize humanitarian visas for them. Once the order went into effect, Luiz and Gis began negotiating the procedures with the embassy in Pakistan.

After three and a half months, eighty-seven Afghan refugees smuggled out of Afghanistan, thanks to the Brazilian missionary couple, finally boarded a plane to São Paulo. They included Hussain, the pizza-delivery employees, the schoolteachers and (Muslim) housekeeper, and the chowkidar with their entire extended families. At the International Airport in São Paulo-Guarulhos, they were welcomed by the organization with which Homero Azis served, +MAIS, which had paid for the tickets and arranged two buses to take them to the southern state of Paraná, where the organization had built a shelter to house all the families while they learned Portuguese.

I went to visit them, and as I arrived, Hussain came toward me and gave me a hug. "It is good to see you safe," I told him. "Who would imagine that we would meet one day in Brazil?" He gave me a big smile. "God has His own ways." After months, the Afghan families were each sent to different cities in Brazil, where they were expected to rebuild their lives with the help of the evangelical churches who sponsored them. Some later moved somewhere else, while others tried to further migrate to the US.

Hussain, perhaps Luiz and Gis's most loyal disciple, died of leukemia on May 11, 2023. When the doctors in Brazil informed him that he didn't have a lot of time left, Hussain confessed his last wish to the church: to return to his beloved homeland. He is buried in Afghanistan. I called Gis to pay my condolences and asked how she was coping. "Well, sad for the loss, but happy for him because his real life has just begun and he is now with the Lord," she told me. "We live with our eyes on eternity, you know." I could hear Luiz's voice in the distance, in agreement. "*É desse jeito!*"

John Corrigan, Melani McAlister, and Axel R. Schäfer (eds.), *Global Faith, Worldly Power: Evangelical Internationalism and U.S. Empire* (University of North Carolina Press, 2018).

Frances FitzGerald, *The Evangelicals: The Struggle to Shape America* (Simon & Schuster, 2017).

Eliza Griswold, *The Tenth Parallel: Dispatches from the Fault Line Between Christianity and Islam* (Farrar, Straus and Giroux, 2010).

Jeffrey Haynes, *Religious Transnational Actors and Soft Power* (Routledge, 2012).

Philip Jenkins, *The Next Christendom: The Coming of Global Christianity* (Oxford University Press, 2002).

Melani McAlister, *The Kingdom of God Has No Borders: A Global History of American Evangelicals* (Oxford University Press, 2018).

Mark A. Noll, *The New Shape of World Christianity: How American Experience Reflects Global Faith* (IVP Academic, 2009).

Dana L. Robert, *Christian Mission: How Christianity Became a World Religion* (Blackwell Brief Histories of Religion) (Wiley-Blackwell, 2009).

Lamin Sanneh, *Disciples of All Nations: Pillars of World Christianity* (Oxford University Press, 2008).

Brian Stanley, *Christianity in the Twentieth Century: A World History* (The Princeton History of Christianity) (Princeton University Press, 2018).

Brian Stanley, *The Global Diffusion of Evangelicalism: The Age of Billy Graham and John Stott* (IVP Academic, 2013).

Ian Tyrrell, *Reforming the World: The Creation of America's Moral Empire* (Princeton University Press, 2010).

Andrew Walls, *The Missionary Movement in Christian History: Studies in the Transmission of Faith* (Orbis Books, 1996).

Robert Wuthnow, *Boundless Faith: The Global Outreach of American Churches* (University of California Press, 2010).

INTRODUCTION

12 **Soldiers described Diyala as the most dangerous and "war-like":** Jamie Tarabay, "Iraq Commander Shares Sentiments on Troops," NPR, November 30, 2007, https://www.npr.org/templates/story/story.php?storyId=16763721.

12 **The vulnerability of the convoys had become apparent:** Dexter Filkins, "Endless Supply Convoy Is Frustrated Endlessly," *New York Times*, March 28, 2003, https://www.nytimes.com/2003/03/28/world/nation-war-field-central-iraq-endless-supply-convoy-frustrated-endlessly.html.

12 **the surge deployed troops into even more dangerous terrains:** Michael Abramowitz and Robin Wright, "Bush to Add 21,500 Troops in an Effort to Stabilize Iraq," *Washington Post*, January 11, 2007, https://www.washingtonpost.com/archive/politics/2007/01/11/bush-to-add-21500-troops-in-an-effort-to-stabilize-iraq/58109e24-a4f3-4700-bf66-9358a8e670f4.

12 **the war's deadliest year for American soldiers:** "2007 Was Deadliest Year for U.S. Troops in Iraq," Associated Press, December 31, 2007, https://www.nbcnews.com/id/wbna22451069.

13 **Casualties among civilians working for private contractors alongside the US military:** James M. Broder and James Risen, "Contractor Deaths in Iraq Soar to Record," *New York Times*, May 19, 2007, https://www.nytimes.com/2007/05/19/world/middleeast/19contractors.html.

13 **caught in an ambush:** Ernesto Londoño, "20 U.S. Troops Killed in Iraq Day Is 3rd Worst Since War Began," *Washington Post*, January 21, 2007, https://www.washingtonpost.com/archive/politics/2007/01/21/20-us-troops-killed-in-iraq-span-classbankheadday-is-3rd-worst-since-war-beganspan/42aca7b8-a0dd-4581-9c70-30d65e47531c; Michael O'Hanlon and Ian S. Livingston, "Iraq Index: Tracking Variables of Reconstruction & Security in Post-Saddam Iraq," The Brookings Institution, December 21, 2007, http://www.brookings.edu/iraqindex.

14 **religious and ethnic violence:** Amina Ismail, "Iraqis Recount Their Struggles After Saddam Hussein's Fall," Reuters, March 15, 2023, https://www.reuters.com/world/middle-east/iraqis-recount-their-struggles-after-saddam-husseins-fall-2023-03-15.

14 **evangelical Protestants**: The term *evangelical* derives from the Greek word *evangelion*, meaning "gospel" or "good news," and it consists of distinctive theological

convictions that came to define a subcategory of mostly conservative Protestants called evangelicals. Those are, according to the most widely accepted definition, by historian David Bebbington, a life-transforming conversion, biblical inerrancy, activism (sharing the gospel), and crucicentrism, the belief that the sacrifice of Jesus Christ on the cross provided atonement for sinful humankind. Though Bebbington's definition has been debated, it is still used by the National Association of Evangelicals, and throughout this book. See David W. Bebbington, *Evangelicalism in Modern Britain: A History from the 1730s to the 1930s* (London: Unwin Hyman, 1989). For a recent reflection on the meaning of *evangelical*, see Mark A. Noll, David Bebbington, and George M. Marsden, *Evangelicals : Who They Have Been, Are Now, and Could Be* (Grand Rapids, Michigan: William B. Eerdmans Publishing Company, 2019).

16 **the Roman Catholic Church:** Though other Christians might identify as Catholics, the term is used throughout this book to refer exclusively to those in communion and under the authority of the pope, as bishop of Rome.

16 **Open Doors, advertised as "the world's largest outreach to persecuted Christians in the most high-risk places":** Andre Mitchell, "Christian Women Suffer More from Persecution Compared to Men, Global Survey Reveals," Christian Today, April 27, 2016, https://www.christiantoday.com/article/christian-women-suffer-more-from-persecution-compared-to-men-global-survey-reveals/84850.htm.

17 **beheaded, stoned, and crucified corpses:** "UN: More Reports of Children Crucified, Beheaded & Stoned to Death by IS," Radio Free Europe/Radio Liberty, December 16, 2014, https://www.rferl.org/a/under-black-flag-un-children-islamic-state/26747119.html.

17 **highest recorded since World War II:** "UNHCR Global Trends 2013," United Nations High Commissioner for Refugees, June 2014, https://www.unhcr.org/media/unhcr-global-trends-2013.

17 **dead bodies were being dug up from the ruins:** Rikar Hussein and Kawa Omar, "Mosul Workers Still Pulling Bodies from Rubble, 6 Months After IS Expulsion," Voice of America, January 26, 2018, https://www.voanews.com/a/mosul-workers-still-pulling-bodies-from-rubble-six-months-after-is-explusion/4227460.html.

18 **"to the ends of the Earth,"** This quote is from Acts 1:8 in the Bible: "But you will receive power when the Holy Spirit comes on you; and you will be my witnesses in

Jerusalem, and in all Judea and Samaria, and to the ends of the Earth."

19 **I kept his complete name secret for safety reasons:** Most Christian missionaries I interviewed in majority-Muslim countries operate in secrecy under code names and asked to be referred to accordingly in the book. I agreed, as long as I knew and was able to confirm their real identities. Like Hannelie and Werner Groenewald, S. P. Luiz and Gis used real identities in Afghanistan, but requested not to have their full names disclosed for their own safety and that of the missionaries to Muslims that they serve in the Middle East and Asia.

19 **iconic cover page in 1966:** John Elson, "Toward a Hidden God," *Time* magazine, April 8, 1966, https://content.time.com/time/subscriber/article/0,33009,835309,00.html.

19 **resurgence of religion as a significant force:** Scott M. Thomas, *The Global Resurgence of Religion and the Transformation of International Relations: The Struggle for the Soul of the Twenty-First Century* (Palgrave Macmillan, 2005). For previous works on the global resurgence of religion, beginning in the late twentieth century, see Peter L. Berger, *The Desecularization of the World: Resurgent Religion and World Politics* (Wm. B. Eerdmans Publishing Co., 1999), p. 6.

19 **experiencing religious revivals:** Eleanor Albert, "Christianity in China," Council on Foreign Relations, October 11, 2018, https://www.cfr.org/backgrounder/christianity-china; Neha Sahgal, Jonathan Evans, Ariana Monique Salazar, Kelsey Jo Starr, and Manolo Corichi, "Religion in India: Tolerance and Segregation," Pew Research Center, June 29, 2021, https://www.pewresearch.org/religion/2021/06/29/religion-in-india-tolerance-and-segregation.

20 **Christianity's shift to the Global South:** "The Changing Global Religious Landscape," Pew Research Center, April 5, 2017, https://www.pewresearch.org/religion/2017/04/05/the-changing-global-religious-landscape; Wes Granberg-Michaelson, "Think Christianity Is Dying? No, Christianity Is Shifting Dramatically," *Washington Post*, May 20, 2015, https://www.washingtonpost.com/news/acts-of-faith/wp/2015/05/20/think-christianity-is-dying-no-christianity-is-shifting-dramatically; Philip Jenkins, *The Next Christendom: The Coming of Global Christianity* (2002).

20 **over 1.2 billion Christians in Latin America and sub-Saharan Africa:** "Religious Composition by

 Country, 2010–2050," Pew Research Center, 2020.

20 **Catholics still make up half of all Christians worldwide:** "5 Facts About Protestants Around the World," Pew Research Center, https://www.pewresearch.org/fact-tank/2017/10/27/500-years-after-the-reformation-5-facts-about-protestants-around-the-world/.

20 **The force behind the trend is Pentecostalism:** David Martin, *Tongues of Fire: The Explosion of Protestantism in Latin America* (Oxford: Basil Blackwell, 1990), p. 72.

21 **fastest-growing religious sect:** Harvey Cox, *Fire from Heaven: The Rise of Pentecostal Spirituality and the Reshaping of Religion in the Twenty-first Century* (Da Capo Press, 1995).

21 **almost nine in ten of the world's Protestants lived outside of Europe:** "5 Facts About Protestants Around the World."

22 **global missions movement:** Melissa Steffan, "The Surprising Countries Most Missionaries Are Sent From and Go To," *Christianity Today*, July 25, 2013, https://www.christianitytoday.com/news/2013/july/missionaries-countries-sent-received-csgc-gordon-conwell.html.

PROLOGUE

25 **first Bible ever printed in America:** "The Eliot Indian Bible: The First Bible Printed in America," Library of Congress, https://www.loc.gov/exhibits/bibles/interactives/more/other13.html.

25 **The First Great Awakening:** Mark A. Noll, *The Rise of Evangelicalism: The Age of Edwards, Whitefield and the Wesleys* (InterVarsity Press, 2003).

27 **"reconnoiter South America as a missionary field":** James Barnett Taylor, *Memoir of Rev. Luther Rice, One of the First American Missionaries to the East* (1840).

27 **stirred a paradigm shift in missionary thinking:** Edward L. Smither, *Brazilian Evangelical Missions Among Arabs: History, Culture, Practice, and Theology* (dissertation, University of Pretoria, 2010), pp. 57–58, https://digitalcommons.liberty.edu/fac_dis/115.

27 **propelled US missions to Latin America:** Guillermo Cook refers to this development as the beginning of "traditional missions" in Brazil and Latin America. See Guillermo Cook, *The Expectation of the Poor: Latin American Base: Ecclesial Communities in Protestant Perspective* (Wipf & Stock, 1985), p. 44; Edward L. Smither, *Brazilian*

Evangelical Missions among Arabs, p. 57.

27 **The American Bible Society began working in South America soon after its foundation in 1816:** See Antônio Mendonça, "A History of Christianity in Brazil: An Interpretive Essay," p. 382; Tucker, a Bible Society representative in Brazil from 1886–1900, provides helpful insights into a colporteur's experience in his work *The Bible in Brazil*: "Methodist and Episcopal missionaries and their helpers are following up the colporteurs . . ."; Edward L. Smither, *Brazilian Evangelical Missions Among Arabs*, p. 40.

27 **all shared a theological horizon characterized as evangelical:** Edward L. Smither, *Brazilian Evangelical Missions Among Arabs*, p. 58; James C. Fletcher, *Brazil and the Brazilians: Portrayed in Historical and Descriptive Sketches* (Boston: Little, Brown, and Co., 1866).

29 **American Cemetery in Santa Bârbara D'Oeste:** Simon Romero, "A Slice of the Confederacy in the Interior of Brazil," May 8, 2016, https://www.nytimes.com/2016/05/09/world/americas/a-slice-of-the-confederacy-in-the-interior-of-brazil.html.

30 **first national Summer Bible Conference:** "First Summer Bible Conference—1886," Boston University Center for Global Christianity and Mission, https://www.bu.edu/cgcm/2012/06/06/first-summer-bible-conference-1886.

31 **catalyst for American foreign missions:** Steve Shadrach, "The Story of the Student Volunteer Movement," Campus Ministry Today, November 26, 2018, https://campusministry.org/article/the-story-of-the-student-volunteer-movement.

31 **Evangelizing Catholic Latin America concerned the movement's leadership:** Edward L. Smither, *Brazilian Evangelical Missions Among Arabs*, p. 60.

32 **Speer considered the moral conditions in the subcontinent irreligious**. Samuel Escobar, *Changing Tides: Latin America and World Mission Today* (Orbis Books, 2002), p. 25; Guillermo Cook, *The Expectation of the Poor*, p. 44; Robert Speer, *South American Problems* (New York: Student Volunteer Movement for Volunteer Missions, 1912).

32 **"The day has come":** John F. Piper, *Robert E. Speer: Prophet of the American Church* (2000).

34 **Graham held a revival:** "An Evangelistic Meeting on the Steps of the Capitol," Associated Press, February 4, 1952, https://www.nytimes.com/1952/02/04

 /archives/an-evangelistic-meeting-on-the-steps-of-the-capitol.html.

35 **San Lorenzo soccer stadium:** "Crisis Evangelism in Latin America," *Christianity Today*, November 23, 1962, https://www.christianitytoday.com/ct/1962/november-23/crisis-evangelism-in-latin-america.html.

35 **Second Vatican Council:** Jordan G. Teicher, "Why Is Vatican II So Important?" NPR, October 10, 2012, https://www.npr.org/2012/10/10/162573716/why-is-vatican-ii-so-important.

36 **revival led by African American holiness preacher William Seymour:** Kevin Sack, "The Pentecostal Church in America," *New York Times*, June 4, 2000, https://archive.nytimes.com/www.nytimes.com/library/national/race/060400sack-church-side.html.

36 **Gunnar Vingren and Daniel Berg:** Justo L. González and Ondina E. González, *Christianity in Latin America: A History* (2008), 282.

37 **a warm welcome in Latin America:** See Samuel Escobar, *Changing Tides*, pp. 55, 56, 81; Juan Sepúlveda, "The Pentecostal Movement in Latin America," in Guillermo Cook (ed.) *New Face of the Church in Latin America: Between Tradition and Change* (Maryknoll, NY: Orbis Books, 1994); Cecília Mariz, "Religion and Poverty in Brazil: A Comparison of Catholic and Pentecostal Communities," *Sociology of Religion* 53 (1992), https://doi.org/10.2307/3711251; Harvey Cox, *Fire from Heaven* (New York: Addison-Wesley, 1995).

37 **Influenced by Pentecostalism:** Leonildo Silveira Compos, for example, points to "Pentecostalized Protestantism" and "Protestantized Pentecostalism." Leonildo Silveira Campos, "Why Historic Churches Are Declining and Pentecostal Churches Are Growing in Brazil," in *In the Power of the Spirit: The Pentecostal Challenge to Historic Churches in Latin America* (Presbyterian Church [U.S.A.], Worldwide Ministries Division, 1996), p. 92.

37 **charismatic movement:** In fact, the two terms—*Protestant* and *Evangelical*—are used interchangeably in Latin America while Catholics who adhered to Pentecostal beliefs and practices are called Charismatic.

37 **liberation theology:** Guillermo Cook, *The Expectation of the Poor*. The term *liberation theology* itself appears to have been coined by Brazilian Presbyterian Rubem Alves (1933–2014) and Argentinian Methodist José Míguez Bonino (1924–2012), who attended the Second Vatican Council and CELAM in Medellin as an observer invited by Pope Paul VI. A lot about liberation theology

here comes from Sherron K. George, "Brazil: An 'Evangelized' Giant Calling for Liberating Evangelism," *International Bulletin of Missionary Research* 26, no. 3 (July 2002).

37 ***communidades eclesyasticas de base*:** Jose Comblin, "Brazil: Base Communities in the Northeast," in *New Face of the Church in Latin America*, ed. Guillermo Cook (Maryknoll, NY: Orbis Books, 1994), p. 217.

37 **estimated one hundred thousand in Brazil:** Alan Riding, "Latin Church in Siege," *New York Times*, May 6, 1979, https://www.nytimes.com/1979/05/06/archives/latin-church-in-siege-priests.html; Manuel A. Vasquez, *The Brazilian Popular Church and the Crisis of Modernity* (Cambridge: Cambridge University Press, 1998), pp. 46, 58.

38 **Lausanne, Switzerland, in the summer of 1974:** Brian Stanley, *The Global Diffusion of Evangelicalism: The Age of Billy Graham and John Stott* (2013), 163–167.

40 **"data-oriented church growth school":** "The Spirit of Lausanne," *Christianity Today*, August 30, 1974, https://www.christianitytoday.com/ct/1974/august-30/spirit-of-lausanne.html.

42 **"The terms of the next forty years":** Melani McAlister, "The Global Conscience of American Evangelicalism: Internationalism and Social Concern in the 1970s and Beyond," *Journal of American Studies* (November 2017), 1197–1220.

45 **10 and 40 degrees latitude north of the equator:** Luis Bush, "The Challenge Before Us," Lausanne Movement, https://lausanne.org/wp-content/uploads/2007/06/058.pdf.

CHAPTER ONE

47 **colony's first slave rebellion:** Glenn Cheney, *Quilombo Dos Palmares: Brazil's Lost Nation of Fugitive Slaves* (2016).

49 **sparked an international backlash:** Edward Rhodes, "Onward, Liberal Soldiers? The Crusading Logic of Bush's Grand Strategy and What Is Wrong with It," in *The New American Empire: A 21st Century Teach-In on U.S. Foreign Policy*, edited by Lloyd C. Gardner and Marilyn B. Young (2005), 228–252.

50 **"a higher father that I appeal to":** Bob Woodward, *Plan of Attack* (2004).

50 **"helped sell Americans the Iraq War":** Brian Murphy, "Michael Gerson, Post Columnist and Bush Speechwriter on 9/11, Dies at 58," *Washington Post*, November 17, 2022, https://www.washingtonpost

.com/obituaries/2022/11/17/michael-gerson-speechwriter-post-dies.

50 **"wicked" and "evil religion":** Stephen Prothero, "Billy Graham Built a Movement. Now His Son Is Dismantling It," *Politico Magazine*, February 24, 2018, https://www.politico.com/magazine/story/2018/02/24/billy-graham-evangelical-decline-franklin-graham-217077.

50 **"not a peaceful religion":** "Islam Is Violent in Nature, Pat Robertson Says," Associated Press, February 23, 2002, https://www.nytimes.com/2002/02/23/us/nation-challenged-religious-right-islam-violent-nature-pat-robertson-says.html.

51 **"I agree that there is evil":** Tony Carnes, "The Bush Doctrine," *Christianity Today*, May 1, 2003, https://www.christianitytoday.com/ct/2003/may/3.38.html.

51 **missionaries in Islamic countries quadrupled:** Deborah Caldwell, "Should Christian Missionaries Heed the Call in Iraq?" *New York Times*, April 6, 2003, https://www.nytimes.com/2003/04/06/weekinreview/the-nation-should-christian-missionaries-heed-the-call-in-iraq.html.

52 **most pervasive global evangelical network:** John Lambert, "Massive Prayer and Missions Movements of the 90s," *Lifestyle of Prayer*, July 2014, https://www.missionfrontiers.org/issue/article/massive-prayer-and-missions-movements-of-the-90s.

52 **push to proselytize to Muslims:** J. Dudley Woodberry, "Missions in the Muslim World—A Decade After 9/11," Asia Missions Advance, April 2012, https://www.asiamissions.net/wp-content/uploads/2014/08/ama_35.pdf; David Van Biema, "Missionaries Under Cover, *Time* magazine, June 30, 2003, https://content.time.com/time/subscriber/article/0,33009,1005107,00.html.

53 **a yearlong investigation:** Farah Stockman, Michael Kranish, Peter S. Canellos, and Kevin Baron, "Bush Brings Faith to Foreign Aid: As Funding Rises, Christian Groups Deliver Help—with a Message," *Boston Globe*, October 8, 2006, http://archive.boston.com/news/special/faith_based/faith_based_organizations_alphaup.htm.

54 **International Federation of Red Cross and Red Crescent Societies code of conduct:** Annex VI: The Code of Conduct for the International Red Cross and Red Crescent Movement and NGOs in Disaster Relief, 29-02-1996 Article, International Review of the Red Cross, No. 310, https://www.icrc.org/en/doc/resources/documents/article/other/code-of-conduct-290296.htm.

55 **Martin and Gracia Burnham:** "U.S. Hostage Dead in Philippines," ABC News, June 7, 2002, https://abcnews.go.com/International/story?id=79955.

55 **presence of American missionaries:** Susan Sachs, "With Missionaries Spreading, Muslims' Anger Is Following," *New York Times*, December 31, 2002, https://www.nytimes.com/2002/12/31/world/threats-responses-religion-with-missionaries-spreading-muslims-anger-following.html.

55 **growing concern with the presence of American missionaries in the field:** Darrell L. Bock, "The State of Missions: Interview with Luis Bush," Associated Press, July 1, 2003, https://www.christianitytoday.com/ct/2003/july/19.26.html.

56 **"Somebody is going to have to risk their life to bring the Gospel to the Yemenites":** G. Jeffrey MacDonald, "Missionaries Adjust to Risks in Arab Lands," *Christian Science Monitor*, February 20, 2003, https://www.csmonitor.com/2003/0220/p13s01-lire.html.

56 **Bush presented the complete findings:** Luis Bush, "World Inquiry Purpose Process People Paradigm Emerging," Luis Bush Papers, https://luisbushpapers.com/world-inquiry/2002/03/01/world-inquiry-purpose-process-people-paradigm-emerging.

56 **read a conference paper:** "Lausanne Occasional Paper: The Two Thirds World Church," Lausanne Movement, 2004, https://lausanne.org/content/lop/two-thirds-world-church-lop-44.

CHAPTER TWO

65 **resumed his ministry:** Scott Baldauf, "Christian Aid Worker Back in Kabul," *Christian Science Monitor*, August 29, 2002, https://www.csmonitor.com/2002/0829/p01s04-wosc.html.

70 **"the invading Americans":** Jonathon Burch and Rob Taylor, "Afghan Taliban Declare Start to Spring Offensive," Reuters, April 29, 2011, https://www.reuters.com/article/us-afghanistan-taliban/afghan-taliban-declare-start-to-spring-offensive-idUSTRE73T0JU20110430.

70 **mock trial of the Koran:** Camille Mann, "Pastor Terry Jones Receiving Death Threats After Quran Burning," CBS News, April 4, 2011, https://www.cbsnews.com/news/pastor-terry-jones-receiving-death-threats-after-quran-burning.

71 **deadliest attack on the UN:** "UN Condemns Afghan Quran Protest Killings," Al Jazeera, April 1, 2011, https://www.aljazeera.com/news/2011/4/1/un-condemns-afghan-quran-protest-killings.

72 **gunned down in broad daylight:** Jenny Percival, "British Aid Worker Shot Dead in Afghanistan 'For Spreading Christianity,'" *The Guardian*, https://www.theguardian.com/world/2008/oct/20/afghanistan-internationalaidanddevelopment.

75 **anti-American riots:** Carlotta Gall, "Anti-U.S. Rioting Erupts in Kabul; at Least 14 Dead," *New York Times*, May 30, 2006, https://www.nytimes.com/2006/05/30/world/asia/30afghan.html.

84 **board a plane with nearly six kilograms of heroin:** "Afghanistan Jails South African for 16 Years Over Drugs," Reuters, October 28, 2008, https://www.reuters.com/article/uk-afghan-drugs/afghanistan-jails-south-african-for-16-years-over-drugs-idUKTRE49R47Y20081028.

93 **Dutch citizen was detained:** "International Religious Freedom Report 2010," Bureau of Democracy, Human Rights, and Labor, November 17, 2010, https://2009-2017.state.gov/j/drl/rls/irf/2010/148786.htm.

95 **footage of foreigners baptizing Afghans:** Mujib Mashal, "In the Afghan Papers: Proselytizing," *New York Times*, June 8, 2010, https://archive.nytimes.com/atwar.blogs.nytimes.com/2010/06/08/in-the-afghan-papers-proselytizing; Maria Abi-Habib, "TV Host Targets Afghan Women's Shelters," *Wall Street Journal*, August 3, 2010, https://www.wsj.com/articles/SB10001424052748704875004575374984291866528.

96 **having the word *church* in their names:** Sanjeev Miglani, "Western Aid Groups Deny Religious Agenda in Afghanistan," Reuters, June 1, 2010, https://www.reuters.com/article/uk-afghanistan-religion/western-aid-groups-deny-religious-agenda-in-afghanistan-idUKTRE6503AV20100601.

96 **captured and executed:** "Foreign Medical Workers Among 10 Killed in Afghanistan," BBC News, August 7, 2010, https://www.bbc.com/news/world-south-asia-10900338.

97 **attacks on humanitarian aid workers:** Aid Worker Security Database, https://www.aidworkersecurity.org.

97 **raid in the Pakistani military town of Abbottabad:** Nicholas Schmidle, "Getting Bin Laden," *New Yorker*, August 1, 2011, https://www.newyorker.com/magazine/2011/08/08/getting-bin-laden.

CHAPTER THREE

99 **Sixteen of them died:** Luke Harding and Rory Carroll, "Church Massacre Leaves Pakistan in Turmoil," *Guardian*, October 28,

2001, https://www.theguardian.com/world/2001/oct/29/pakistan.rorycarroll.

100 **assassination of Shahbaz Bhatti:** Jane Perlez, "Extremists Are Suspected in Killing of Pakistani Minister," *New York Times*, March 2, 2011, https://www.nytimes.com/2011/03/03/world/asia/03pakistan.html.

100 **Salman Taseer had been shot dead:** Ed Husain, "Explaining the Salman Taseer Murder," Council on Foreign Relations, January 7, 2011, https://www.cfr.org/expert-brief/explaining-salman-taseer-murder.

100 **Asia Bibi, an impoverished Christian mother:** Zehra Abid, "Blasphemy in Pakistan: The Case of Aasia Bibi," Al Jazeera America, June 18, 2015, http://america.aljazeera.com/articles/2015/6/18/blasphemy-in-pakistan-the-case-of-aasia-bibi.html.

101 **Pearl Continental Hotel:** Sabrina Tavernise and Salman Masood, "Bombing Challenges Aid to Pakistan Refugees," *New York Times*, June 10, 2009, https://www.nytimes.com/2009/06/11/world/asia/11pstan.html.

105 **drones to conduct bombings:** "The Drone Papers," Intercept, October 15, 2015, https://theintercept.com/drone-papers.

105 **violent militant upsurge:** Ron Moreau, "Pakistan Is the World's Most Dangerous Country," *Newsweek*, September 4, 2010, https://www.newsweek.com/pakistan-worlds-most-dangerous-country-72033.

106 **Abductions had become endemic:** Annabel Symington, "Splintering of Taliban Fuels Spate of Kidnapping in Pakistan," *Wall Street Journal*, July 30, 2014, https://www.wsj.com/articles/splintering-of-taliban-fuels-1406763390; Ihsanullah Tipu Mehsud, Ismail Khan, and Declan Walsh, "Taliban Gain Foothold in a Pakistani City," *New York Times*, July 27, 2013, https://www.nytimes.com/2013/07/28/world/asia/taliban-gain-foothold-in-a-pakistani-city.html.

106 **kidnapped and forced to marry:** Sara Malm, "Christian Family 'Devastated' After Daughter, 24, Is Kidnapped on the Streets of Pakistan and Forced to Marry a Muslim Man," *Daily Mail*, May 16, 2016, https://www.dailymail.co.uk/news/article-3592938/Christian-woman-kidnapped-streets-Pakistan-forced-marry-Muslim-man.html; Mike Thomson, "Abducted, Shackled and Forced to Marry at 12," BBC, March 9, 2021, https://www.bbc.com/news/stories-56337182.

108 **detonated explosive vests amid the worshippers:** Tim Craig,

"Pakistan's Christians Struggle with Casualties After Bloody Church Bombing Kills 85," *Washington Post*, September 23, 2013, https://www.washingtonpost.com/world/pakistans-christians-struggle-with-dead-wounded-after-bloody-church-bombing-kills-85/2013/09/23/780331da-246a-11e3-9372-92606241ae9c_story.html; Zahir Shah Sherazi, "Twin Church Blasts Claim 80 Lives in Peshawar," Dawn, September 22, 2013, https://www.dawn.com/news/1044668.

CHAPTER FOUR

109 **wielding a machete:** Ryan Dagur, "Child Murder Witnesses to Get Counseling," Union of Catholic Asian News, November 7, 2012, https://www.ucanews.com/news/child-murder-witnesses-to-get-counseling/64240.

109 **site of the triple bombings:** Julie Chernov Hwang and Colin P. Clarke, "20 Years After the Bali Bombings, What Have We Learned?" *Foreign Policy*, October 12, 2022, https://foreignpolicy.com/2022/10/12/bali-bombings-indonesia-20th-anniversary-terrorist-attack-jemaah-islamiyah.

110 **rising religious conservativism in Indonesia:** "Indonesia: After the Wave," *Frontline/World*, June 26, 2007, https://www.pbs.org/frontlineworld/stories/indonesia605/sharia.html.

111 **central catalytic movement for global evangelism:** "The 10/40 Window - Getting to the Core of the Core," Luis Bush Papers, https://luisbushpapers.com/1040window/1996/10/22/1040-window-getting-to-the-core-of-the-core.

111 **Western missionaries declined:** Saba Imtiaz, "A New Generation Redefines What It Means to Be a Missionary," *Atlantic*, March 8, 2018, https://www.theatlantic.com/international/archive/2018/03/young-missionaries/551585.

112 **in "Muslim Ministry and Islamic Studies":** i2 Ministries, https://resources.i2ministries.org/products/christian-apologetics-to-islam-joshua-lingel-mp3-set.

113 **top supplier of halal meat:** Andres Schipani, "Brazil Risks Halal Meat Exports with Israel Embassy Move," *Financial Times*, January 19, 2019, https://www.ft.com/content/40bb730c-1930-11e9-9e64-d150b3105d21.

CHAPTER FIVE

115 **Afghan Christian converts persecuted:** Neyaz Farooquee, "An Afghan Church Grows in Delhi," *New York Times*, July 22, 2013, https://archive.nytimes.com/india

.blogs.nytimes.com/2013/07/22/an-afghan-church-grows-in-delhi.

117 **Campus Crusade:** Mary Rourke, "William R. Bright, 81; Evangelist Founded Campus Crusade," *Los Angeles Times*, July 21, 2003, https://www.latimes.com/archives/la-xpm-2003-jul-21-me-bright21-story.html.

119 **Pul-e-Charki:** Susan Ormiston, "Inside an Afghan prison," *CBC News: The National*, May 16, 2011, https://www.youtube.com/watch?v=trRWmoC-ojA.

120 **winning the hearts and minds:** Gilles Dorronsoro, "The Taliban's Winning Strategy in Afghanistan," Carnegie Endowment for International Peace, June 29, 2009, https://carnegieendowment.org/files/taliban_winning_strategy.pdf.

122 **NATO's combat mission in Afghanistan:** "Statement by the President on the End of the Combat Mission in Afghanistan," National Archives, December 28, 2014, https://obamawhitehouse.archives.gov/the-press-office/2014/12/28/statement-president-end-combat-mission-Afghanistan.

122 **President Ashraf Ghani had just taken office:** Sune Engel Rasmussen, "Afghan President Ashraf Ghani Inaugurated After Bitter Campaign," *Guardian*, September 29, 2014, https://www.theguardian.com/world/2014/sep/29/afghan-president-ashraf-ghani-inaugurated.

124 **Taliban claimed responsibility:** Shaun Smillie and Nashira Davids, "Taliban Kill SA family," *Sunday Times*, December 1, 2014, https://www.timeslive.co.za/news/south-africa/2014-12-01-taliban-kill-sa-family.

125 **fire stopped at Jean-Pierre's bedroom:** Barry Bateman, "'The Murder of My Family Is Part of a Divine Plan,'" Eyewitness News, December 12, 2014, https://ewn.co.za/2014/12/12/Hannelie-Groenewald-The-killing-of-my-family-was-part-of-a-divine-plan.

CHAPTER SIX

128 **gangs of thugs roamed the neighborhood:** Sam Dagher, "Thugs-for-Hire Leave Mark on Protests, Egyptians Say," *Wall Street Journal*, February 9, 2011, https://www.wsj.com/articles/SB10001424052748704364004576132340572089236; "Al Jazeera Says Cairo Office Destroyed by 'Thugs'," Reuters, February 4, 2011, https://www.reuters.com/article/uk-egypt-jazeera/al-jazeera-says-cairo-office-destroyed-by-thugs-idUKTRE7133ZC20110204.

129 **cordon to protect Muslim countrymen:** Anne Alexander, "Egypt's Muslims and Christians Join Hands in Protest," BBC News, February 10, 2011, https://www

.bbc.com/news/world-middle-east-12407793.

130 **often neglected pastorally:** Ted Limpic, "O Movimento Missionário Brasileiro," Estatística Missionários Brasileiros, 2006, https://www.scribd.com/document/457221348/Estatistica-Missionarios-Brasileiros.

132 **pure Protestant evangelical liturgy:** Anthony Shenoda, "Reflections on the (In)Visibility of Copts in Egypt," Jadaliyya, May 18, 2011, https://www.jadaliyya.com/Details/24007.

135 **reaction to the growing presence of Christian missionaries:** Beth Baron, *The Orphan Scandal: Christian Missionaries and the Rise of the Muslim Brotherhood* (2014).

136 **social services to the poor and marginalized:** Michael Birnbaum, "In Egypt, New Power Brings New Challenges for Muslim Brotherhood," *Washington Post*, September 20, 2012, https://www.washingtonpost.com/world/middle_east/in-egypt-new-power-brings-new-challenges-for-muslim-brotherhood/2012/09/19/b239a94c-0279-11e2-8102-ebee9c66e190_story.html.

136 **Alexandria church's New Year service:** David Batty, "Egypt Bomb Kills New Year Churchgoers," *Guardian*, January 1, 2011, https://www.theguardian.com/world/2011/jan/01/egypt-bomb-kills-new-year-churchgoers.

137 **military attacked a Coptic protest:** "Egypt: Don't Cover Up Military Killing of Copt Protesters," Human Rights Watch, October 25, 2011, https://www.hrw.org/news/2011/10/25/egypt-dont-cover-military-killing-copt-protesters.

138 **70 percent of the seats:** David D. Kirkpatrick, "Islamists Win 70% of Seats in the Egyptian Parliament," *New York Times*, January 21, 2012, https://www.nytimes.com/2012/01/22/world/middleeast/muslim-brotherhood-wins-47-of-egypt-assembly-seats.html.

138 **4/14 Movement:** Thomas G. Smoak III, "An Open Window on Brazil," Transform World newsletter, 2012, https://www.transform-world.net/newsletters/2012/414Brazil.pdf.

139 **stormed two camps in Cairo:** Max Fisher, "Egypt's Dictator Murdered 800 People Today in 2013. He's Now a US Ally and GOP Folk Hero," Vox, August 14, 2015, https://www.vox.com/2015/8/14/9153967/rabaa-sisi.

139 **wave of violence against Christians:** Sarah Yerkes, "What Egypt Under Sissi Is Really Like for Coptic Christians," Brookings, June 20, 2016, https://www.brookings.edu/articles/what-egypt-under-sissi-is-really-like-for-coptic-christians.

141 **church in Cairo:** Anna Dowell, "The Church in the Square: Negotiations of Religion and Revolution at an Evangelical Church in Cairo, Egypt," The American University in Cairo, May 2012, https://core.ac.uk/download/pdf/333724256.pdf.

142 **Red Friday Million-Man March:** Ali Al-Raggal, "Four Years Later, Egypt's January 25 Revolution Is Faded Dream," As-Safir Al-Arabi, January 26, 2015, https://assafirarabi.com/en/3246/2015/01/26/four-years-later-egypts-january-25-revolution-is-faded-dream.

143 **Islamic State of Iraq and Syria:** Martin Chulov, "ISIS: The Inside Story," *The Guardian*, December 11, 2014, https://www.theguardian.com/world/2014/dec/11/-sp-isis-the-inside-story.

CHAPTER SEVEN

144 **ten thousand men, women, and children:** Matthew Vickery, "Sea Survivors' Stories: Landing on Lesbos," Al Jazeera, October 21, 2015, https://www.aljazeera.com/features/2015/10/21/sea-survivors-stories-landing-on-lesbos.

145 **left the country and sought asylum:** Adrian Edwards, "Global Forced Displacement Hits Record High," United Nations High Commissioner for Refugees, June 20, 2016, https://www.unhcr.org/us/news/stories/global-forced-displacement-hits-record-high.

146 **boat had sunk off its shores:** "Twelve Migrants Drown as Boat Sinks off Turkey," Al Arabiya, October 17, 2015, https://english.alarabiya.net/News/middle-east/2015/10/17/Twelve-migrants-drown-as-boat-sinks-off-Turkey.

148 **they had almost vanished:** Jane Arraf, "It's a Dangerous Time for Christians in Northeastern Syria," heard on *Morning Edition*, NPR, February 12, 2020, https://www.npr.org/2020/02/12/805154261/its-a-dangerous-time-for-christians-in-northeastern-syria.

149 **Christians in Al-Hasakah had formed a militia:** Jean Aziz, "Syrian Christian Militias Liberate Hasakah," Al-Monitor, October 20, 2015, https://www.al-monitor.com/originals/2015/10/syria-christians-militias-liberation-battle.html.

149 **Ninety residents of the soldier's hometown, primarily elders, were abducted:** Samantha Masunaga, "Relatives Await Word on Assyrians Abducted by Islamic State in Syria," *Los Angeles Times*, February 27, 2015, https://www.latimes.com/world/middleeast/la-fg-syria-christians-20150226-story.html.

150 **genocide of the Yazidis**: Jane Arraf, "Years After a Massacre,

Yazidis Finally Bury Their Loved Ones," *New York Times*, February 7, 2021, https://www.nytimes.com/2021/02/07/world/middleeast/yazidi-funeral-isis-iraq.html.

151 **Christians out of their ancient homelands:** Ruth Sherlock, "Christians Flee Syria Village That Speaks the Language of Jesus," *Telegraph*, September 8, 2013, https://www.telegraph.co.uk/news/worldnews/middleeast/syria/10294711/Christians-flee-Syria-village-that-speaks-the-language-of-Jesus.html; "Syria's Beleaguered Christians," BBC News, February 25, 2015, https://www.bbc.com/news/world-middle-east-22270455.

151 **Nineveh Plain Protection Units:** Balint Szlanko, "Christian Militias Fighting IS in Iraq Hope for US Support," Associated Press, June 16, 2016, https://apnews.com/0fe91066c48641069f22ee96fbdb7a4b.

152 **they had no place at all:** Eliza Griswold, "Is This the End of Christianity in the Middle East?" *New York Times Magazine*, July 22, 2015, https://www.nytimes.com/2015/07/26/magazine/is-this-the-end-of-christianity-in-the-middle-east.html.

CHAPTER EIGHT

156 **Special Immigration Visa:** "Special Immigrant Visas (SIVs) for Iraqi and Afghan Translators/Interpreters," US Department of State, https://travel.state.gov/content/travel/en/us-visas/immigrate/siv-iraqi-afghan-translators-interpreters.html.

157 **Christian Arabic Church of Anaheim:** Christian Arabic Church, https://christianarabic.tithelysetup7.com/about/history.

157 **nearly one-third Iraqi American:** Claire Trageser, "Large Chaldean Iraqi Population Thrives in San Diego Suburb," CalMatters, December 11, 2019, https://calmatters.org/california-divide/2019/12/large-chaldean-iraqi-population-el-cajon.

158 **Christian biweekly magazine *World*:** Sophia Lee, "Friends and Strangers," *World*, August 7, 2015, https://wng.org/articles/friends-and-strangers-1617326624.

158 **suspended immigrants from seven Muslim-majority countries:** "Trump's Executive Order on Immigration, Annotated," NPR, January 31, 2017, https://www.npr.org/2017/01/31/512439121/trumps-executive-order-on-immigration-annotated.

158 **fiercest opposition to the Muslim ban:** Sarah Pulliam Bailey, "Conservative Evangelicals Join Letter Denouncing Trump's Order on Refugees," *Washington Post*, February 8, 2017, https://www.washingtonpost.com/news/acts-of-faith/wp/2017/02/08/conservative-evangelicals

-join-letter-denouncing-trumps -order-on-refugees.

159 **"a sustainable Christian response":** Timothy C. Morgan, "Evangelicals Commit to Refugee Resettlement Efforts," Religion News Service, December 18, 2015, https://www.deseret.com/2015/12/18/20579051/evangelicals-commit-to-refugee-resettlement-efforts.

160 **"reach people who are coming to our shores":** Kate Shellnutt, "Evangelical Experts Oppose Trump's Refugee Ban," *Christianity Today*, January 25, 2017, https://www.christianitytoday.com/news/2017/january/evangelical-experts-oppose-trump-plan-to-ban-refugees-syria.html.

161 **lifeline to these uniquely vulnerable individuals:** Keegan Hamilton, "Evangelical Christian Groups Are Outraged at Trump's Refugee Ban," Vice News, January 30, 2017, https://www.vice.com/en/article/evaekn/evangelical-christian-groups-are-outraged-at-trumps-refugee-ban.

161 **"miss the opportunity":** Kate Shellnutt, "Missionaries Dreamed of This Muslim Moment. Trump's Travel Ban May End It." *Christianity Today*, March 20, 2017, https://www.christianitytoday.com/news/2017/march/missionaries-muslim-moment-trump-travel-ban.html.

162 **obligation to refugees:** Hannah Hartig, "Republicans Turn More Negative Toward Refugees as Number Admitted to U.S. Plummets," Pew Research Center, May 24, 2018, https://www.pewresearch.org/short-reads/2018/05/24/republicans-turn-more-negative-toward-refugees-as-number-admitted-to-u-s-plummets; Gregory A. Smith, "Most White Evangelicals Approve of Trump Travel Prohibition and Express Concerns About Extremism," Pew Research Center, February 27, 2017, https://www.pewresearch.org/short-reads/2017/02/27/most-white-evangelicals-approve-of-trump-travel-prohibition-and-express-concerns-about-extremism.

164 **the increasingly diverse:** Sarah Eekhoff Zylstra, "1 in 3 American Evangelicals Is a Person of Color," *Christianity Today*, September 6, 2017, https://www.christianitytoday.com/news/2017/september/1-in-3-american-evangelicals-person-of-color-prri-atlas.html.

165 **Diversity within congregations has been growing:** Kevin D. Dougherty, Mark Chaves, and Michael O. Emerson, "Racial Diversity in U.S. Congregations, 1998–2019," *Journal for the Scientific Study of Religion* (October 2020).

166 **white evangelical Protestants voted for Trump:** Mehdi Hasan, "Many White Evangelicals Stand by Trump Because They Are More White Than Evangelical," *New Statesman*, December 7, 2017, https://www.newstatesman.com/world/2017/12/many-white-evangelicals-stand-trump-because-they-are-more-white-evangelical; Joe Carter, "No, the Majority of American Evangelicals Did Not Vote for Trump," The Gospel Coalition, November 15, 2016, https://www.thegospelcoalition.org/article/no-the-majority-of-american-evangelicals-did-not-vote-for-trump.

166 **chanting "Christ is king":** Jack Jenkins, "Faith Leaders Ask Why Jan. 6 Report Left Out Christian Nationalism," *Washington Post*, December 29, 2022, https://www.washingtonpost.com/religion/2022/12/29/jan-6-report-christian-nationalism.

EPILOGUE

167 **Taliban had taken control of Jalalabad:** "Taliban Seizes Afghanistan's Jalalabad, Cuts Off Kabul From East," Al Jazeera, August 15, 2021, https://www.aljazeera.com/news/2021/8/15/taliban-capture-afghanistans-jalalabad-cut-off-kabul-from-east.

167 **America's longest war:** Steve Coll, "Leaving Afghanistan, and the Lessons of America's Longest War," *New Yorker*, April 15, 2021, https://www.newyorker.com/news/daily-comment/leaving-afghanistan-and-the-lessons-of-americas-longest-war.

Columbia Global Reports is a nonprofit publishing imprint from Columbia University that commissions authors to produce works of original thinking and on-site reporting from all over the world, on a wide range of topics. Our books are short—novella-length, and readable in a few hours—but ambitious. They offer new ways of looking at and understanding the major issues of our time. Most readers are curious and busy. Our books are for them.

If this book changed the way you look at the world, and if you would like to support our mission, consider making a gift to Columbia Global Reports to help us share new ideas and stories.

Visit globalreports.columbia.edu to support our upcoming books, subscribe to our newsletter, and learn more about Columbia Global Reports. Thank you for being part of our community of readers and supporters.

Why Flying Is Miserable and How to Fix It
Ganesh Sitaraman

Putin's Exiles: Their Fight for a Better Russia
Paul Starobin

The Lie Detectives: In Search of a Playbook for Winning Elections in the Disinformation Age
Sasha Issenberg

Climate Radicals: Why Our Environmental Politics Isn't Working
Cameron Abadi

Left Adrift: What Happened to Liberal Politics
Timothy Shenk

In Defense of Partisanship
Julian Zelizer